WHEN SCHOOL REFORM GOES WRONG

WHEN SCHOOL REFORM GOES WRONG

Nel Noddings

TEACHERS
COLLEGE
PRESS

Teachers College, Columbia University
New York and London

Published by Teachers College Press, 1234 Amsterdam Avenue, New York, NY 10027

Library of Congress Cataloging-in-Publication Data

Noddings, Nel.
    When school reform goes wrong / Nel Noddings.
        p.   cm.
    Includes bibliographical references and index.
    ISBN 978-0-8077-4810-7 (pbk : alk. paper) — ISBN 978-0-8077-4811-4 (cloth : alk. paper)
    1. Educational change—United States.   2. Educational accountability—United States.   I. Title.

    LA217 .N63 2007
    370.973—dc22

                                                                          2007011048

ISBN 978-0-8077-4810-7 (paper)
ISBN 978-0-8077-4811-4 (cloth)

Printed on acid-free paper
Manufactured in the United States of America

14   13   12   11   10   9   8   7   8   7   6   5   4   3   2   1

CONTENTS

A PREFATORY NOTE

OUR PUBLIC SCHOOLS are under siege. Worries about low test scores and "not enough math and science" have led policymakers to instigate a system that is frighteningly antiintellectual and antidemocratic. We must change this.

This book is not a history of school reform, nor is it a review of empirical research. It is an essay, laying out an argument—an invitation to dialogue and, I hope, to action. There are very few footnotes or parenthetical references to interrupt the flow of argument, but I have included at the end a short list of works for those interested. Some of these writers agree with me; some do not.

I have been in education for more than 50 years—as a teacher (at every level from 5th grade to high school mathematics to graduate school), administrator, teacher educator, and philosopher. I speak from that experience and from a deep concern for teachers and students. I could be wrong, and as I tell my students repeatedly, we should remember that reasonable people may differ on controversial matters. If I am right, however, public education in the United States is in real trouble. For the sake of our kids, our schools, and our democracy, we must grapple with these issues.

WHEN SCHOOL REFORM GOES WRONG

INTRODUCTION

IN THE FIRST decade of the 21st century, American schools find themselves operating under federal rules that some people believe will increase the competence of teachers and the achievement of students. Others believe those same rules are undermining—perhaps destroying—American education. The rules under dispute are incorporated in the No Child Left Behind Act (NCLB), enacted in 2002 as the reauthorization of the Elementary and Secondary Education Act (ESEA) first legislated in 1965, but the spirit of the current reform movement preceded NCLB by more than a decade—increased emphasis on academic coursework, accountability, and standardized testing.

ESEA was promoted as a federal attempt to close the achievement gap between rich and poor by providing needed resources to schools attended by significant numbers of poor children. Today's policymakers express displeasure with the undeniable fact that large achievement gaps remain, and they have made a commitment to specifically target the gap between White and Black/Hispanic achievement. Implicit in the provisions of NCLB is a further displeasure with the ways in which monies available under ESEA have been used. The money for additional resources has not so far produced higher test scores, and NCLB is designed to ensure that federal monies are used effectively—that is, that higher achievement will be the actual result.

In this introduction, I want to invite readers to think critically about the ideas underlying NCLB, the reform movement that shaped it, and the processes it has put into play. Suppose you had been part of the conversation leading up to NCLB. Suppose U.S. policymakers told you that, at the

1

start of the 21st century, they wanted to accomplish two main goals for American education: (1) elimination or reduction of the achievement gap between White students and Black/Hispanic students, and (2) establishment of solid evidence that federal monies are well spent in U.S. schools. What questions would you want to ask before endorsing these goals? I will suggest some questions, and they will provide the structure of analysis for the chapters in this book.

We might start by questioning the assumption that the use of federal money is justified only by raised achievement scores. Are there no other worthy goals that might be attained using federal funds? Suppose, for example, that federal monies were used in our urban schools to repair decrepit school facilities, provide medical and dental clinics on school sites, ensure that every student has a textbook for each subject, and provide a desk and chair for every student in every classroom? Such expenditures might well produce enhanced achievement. However, if they did not, should we conclude that the money has been wasted?

We have known for more than 40 years that physical facilities and services in our urban schools are often below par. Some critics have pointed to such poor conditions as the likely reason for the achievement gap. But this may not be the whole answer. In some states and districts, poor schools have been given large budget increases, and physical conditions are quite good. (This is true, for example, in many of the so-called Abbott schools in New Jersey.) But achievement scores have not risen, and some critics therefore insist that "money is not the answer."

Perhaps money is not the answer—or at least not the complete answer—to raising test scores. But proper facilities and adequate resources should be provided *as a matter of decency*. We do not feed hungry children so that they will do well on tests. We feed them because they are hungry, and it is the decent thing to do. Similarly, we should provide for all children physical conditions and resources that we would be willing to accept for our own children. It is the right thing to do. As we improve conditions for poor students, we can also work to increase achievement, but better conditions should not be contingent upon higher test scores.

We might also ask why if the problem to be solved lies mainly in schools attended by poor children, the solution promoted by NCLB has been laid on all schools. Why are we not concentrating on the identification and analysis of problems in the schools where the problematic situations exist? Policymakers respond to this reasonable question by admitting that the achievement gap is not their only worry. "Our schools are failing," they say. All of them? What is the evidence for this charge?

To support the charge of widespread failure, policymakers often cite *A Nation at Risk*, a 1983 report that declared our schools drowning in "a rising tide of mediocrity." The alarmist language in that report has been challenged by many scholars. Among other complaints, the writers of the report expressed concern about a drop in SAT scores. But reasonable observers will note that the SATs, like all standardized tests, establish norms that are dependent on the population of test takers. When that population increases substantially, it is predictable that the norms—for example, the mean and median—will change. Such changes are built into the very concept of standardized testing. That many more students are taking the SATs may or may not be something to celebrate. That is a different matter.

The report also expressed concern that a smaller proportion of students was enrolling in advanced mathematics, physics, and chemistry. Should we be worried about this? Do all students need these courses? Why? These are serious questions that should induce careful analysis and debate. We might well agree that citizens today should be scientifically literate, but what exactly does this mean? Are traditional, highly specialized courses in physics and chemistry necessary for such literacy? Might they even impede such literacy by discouraging interest in scientific topics?

The report raises a more important point in its observation that there has been a drop in the absolute number of students scoring at the very highest levels on the SATs. If this is true, we might ask whether we are giving enough time and attention to those students who are both able and interested in advanced academic work. Perhaps by forcing all students into courses that are essential for relatively few, we are hurting both those who need the courses and those who could profit from different coursework.

The trend toward requiring all students to take traditional academic courses started before NCLB, as part of the reform movement generated by *A Nation at Risk*, but it is compatible with the standardization of curriculum that accompanies NCLB. Brushing aside profound questions about the aims of education and the different needs of different students, policymakers argue that all students should take the courses once offered to only a few. This requirement is made in the name of equality, and so we will have to spend some time analyzing the concept of equality. Does sameness guarantee equality, or—to the contrary—does it ensure greater inequalities?

Some time ago, I visited a fine independent primary/elementary school. While I was chatting with the principal in her office, a small girl came running into the office, climbed into a vacant chair, and began talking to the principal. It was obvious that this was not an unusual incident, and the principal welcomed the little girl, Hope, warmly. The child was soon followed by her teacher, who also joined in the conversation. Hope, about 4 or 5 years old, has Down syndrome, and it is hard to understand her speech. But what a charmer she is—all smiles and curiosity. Hope is just learning to use the toilet and to speak. I thought, as the conversation proceeded with the teacher helping to interpret, how lucky this child was to be enrolled in a school that welcomed her—one whose faculty and staff delighted in her presence and every sign of progress.

Many special education students in schools regulated by NCLB are expected to meet the same standards as regular students. Hearing this for the first time, most readers/listeners react with astonishment. How can policymakers make such a demand? Some even say, citing equality again, that special education students will feel left out if they are not required to take the same tests as other students. One begins to wonder, on hearing this, whether policymakers have any understanding of children and whether any real thinking has gone into the development of NCLB. The motto seems to be, "Never mind. Just raise the test scores of all children." This mindless attitude is captured in the popular slogan "No excuses!"

As we'll see a bit later, the requirement that special education students meet the standards—whatever they are—represents a high-stakes threat to both students and schools. In some states, children who fail a high-stakes test are retained in grade. In all states, schools (with a statistically significant number of special education students) in which those students do not meet the standards are evaluated as failing to have made adequate yearly progress (AYP). The stakes are high, not only for students and schools but also for administrators, who may lose their jobs. It is not surprising that administrators are trying all sorts of strategies, some of them ethically questionable, to avoid the perceived failure of their special education students.

On a visit to an elementary school in Detroit, I was waiting near the office door for the school's principal. A small boy came out of the office clutching a cloth pad to his jaw. A sympathetic secretary in the office responded to my question about this with a laconic, "Toothache. It happens every day." And I wondered how this youngster might respond to his arithmetic lesson of the day. No excuses? This slogan represents mindlessness at its most egregious. The child needs dental work, not more expert instruction in mathematics.

When we *think* about what is demanded of our schools today, we may begin to suspect that the demands are at least in part an attempt to distract citizens from the social problems that plague our cities and some depressed rural areas. Never mind that children are housed badly, that they need medical and dental attention, that they may live in fear of violence, that a parent may be imprisoned or abused. Never mind. No excuses. Just raise the test scores.

The point of using test scores as the measure of achievement is to hold schools, teachers, and students accountable. Every teacher's performance must be accounted for, and every score becomes part of the record of accountability. To be sure that the demand for accountability is taken seriously, penalties and sanctions have been instituted. Schools must demonstrate that they have made "adequate yearly progress" toward the goal of 100% proficiency by 2014; that is, it is demanded that by the year 2014 every student must be proficient in reading and mathematics. A school that fails to make AYP suffers increasingly stiff penalties over a period of 5 years. Students who do not pass the standardized tests in a given year may be retained in grade or fail to graduate from high school. (Use of this penalty varies from state to state. Some states retain many students; other states rarely invoke that penalty.) Teachers and administrators in failing schools may be transferred or even fired. Thus the tests ensuring accountability are "high- stakes tests."

A host of questions may now arise from thoughtful readers and participants in the conversation. Should educators be accountable only for test scores? Should they not be accountable for the means used to get high scores? If students hate learning and teachers are demoralized, should not someone be accountable for these effects? Should schools be accountable only for specific learning outcomes, or should they also be accountable for what is offered? The move from emphasis on inputs to emphasis on outputs (or outcomes) is understandable; we should want to know more about the effects of our efforts. But a measure of inputs is vital; it is, in part, a measure of opportunities offered. Should we try to document valuable learning that has occurred even though it was not prespecified? Should we worry about the diminished curriculum that often results from concentration on prespecified standards? All of these questions will be addressed in some depth in the chapter on accountability.

If schools are to be held accountable for test scores, we should ask what will be on those tests. Here more worries arise. The practice now widespread in schools, especially poor/minority schools is to teach all and only the material to be tested. Teachers cannot, of course, teach specific test items, but they are directed to connect every lesson to a specified standard. These standards, as described in the current reform movement, are statements of content. As Diane Ravitch explains, "Content standards (or curriculum standards) describe what teachers are supposed to teach and students are expected to learn" (1995, p. 12). Most advocates of the current reform movement insist on a high degree of specificity for standards. Teachers must know exactly what they should teach, and students must know exactly what they should learn. Notice that, under such a system, we can usually answer the question, Has Johnny learned X?—but we cannot answer the far more interesting question, What has Johnny learned? There is no encouragement in this system to invite students to follow different interests with respect to broad topics or to support teachers in presenting exciting material that may or may not be learned. We'll say much more about this in the chapter on standards.

Intelligent readers may respond to this description of standards with a mixture of discomfort and tolerance. They may complain that this is not what we usually mean by *standard*. In a more familiar use of the term, we first have a design, proposed product, or mass of content, and then we consider the standard that each of these or the associated workers producing them should meet. But perhaps a set of content standards as presently conceived can serve as a standard curriculum? To this degree we may be tolerant. But our discomfort returns when we consider the advisability of one standard curriculum. How can this possibly serve the interests and needs of all students? Might it smother initiative and imagination? We'll discuss this problem in some depth.

In addition to content standards, schools must have performance standards, and it is on the basis of student performance that schools and teachers will be judged. NCLB allows each state to set its own performance standards. Whether this is appropriate or bizarre is an open question. In a nation that still respects the rights of a state to supervise the schooling of its citizens, it seems appropriate. In conjunction with other provisions of NCLB, it is bizarre. For example, a student who is judged failing in New Mexico might become instantly proficient if his family moves across the border into Colorado. Is the solution, then, national proficiency standards? We will see that there are many reasons to move slowly on this.

A third type of standard is mentioned—opportunity-to-learn standards. These standards are meant to describe the conditions, resources, and modes of delivery that must be available in order for students and teachers to meet performance standards. Expressing a professed unwillingness to intrude on states' right to run their own schools, the federal government says little about the provision of adequate resources. A skeptic may well feel another twinge of discomfort. Considering the massive intrusions present in NCLB, can government policymakers be serious in their reluctance to prescribe the physical conditions of schooling? Or is there a real fear that providing adequate resources will require federal money? Never mind. No excuses. The present thinking on opportunity to learn equates opportunity with exposure to one standard curriculum. If all children have the same curriculum and a highly qualified teacher (we'll have to discuss this), then they supposedly have an equal opportunity to learn.

NCLB does require certain safety standards, and schools must report on the number of cases of vandalism, fighting, sexual harassment, and other infractions that threaten the safety of students, but again the most profound questions are ignored. We should ask why so many protections are needed today—protections that were unheard of 50 years ago. Why is it that high schools 50 years ago did not need security guards, metal detectors (even if they had been available), locked exits, silent corridors, 20-minute lunch "hours," and the like? Instead of asking these questions, we are urged to employ more protective devices, zero-tolerance rules, and stricter penalties. In discussing these issues, I will not suggest that we can turn the clock back 50 years but rather that we should ask basic questions and probe them deeply. Is it possible to get at the causes of the problems that require the current protections? Can anything be done about these underlying problems?

Because NCLB puts so much emphasis on tests, we will have to consider that topic carefully. How often should tests be given? To whom? How should the results be reported? Should alternative methods of evaluation be considered? How should the progress of youngsters like Hope, the child with Down syndrome, be evaluated? What are the costs associated with testing, and might this money be better spent? Tests must be constructed and field tested. Should tests be designed to fit the curriculum, or should tests be allowed to determine the curriculum? It also costs money to buy the tests, administer and monitor them, score them, disaggregate the scores, analyze them, and gather everything into a publicly accessible (and standard) form. Should we count the cost in work-hours to do all this? The people who work in the area of testing are often paid more than the loving teacher who works creatively and patiently with Hope. Are we spending our money wisely?

One reason for using test scores as the main criterion of AYP and of accountability in general is that they are easily obtained, supposedly objective, and yield nicely to statistical analysis and reporting charts. But those very attributes make them susceptible to manipulation, and there is rising concern about cheating. There are reports of cheating by students, teachers, and administrators. Apparently, data are also sometimes manipulated in district offices, and a considerable amount of time is spent on locating loopholes and figuring out ways to meet the letter of the law. If these reports are validated, we will have to conclude that NCLB is a corrupting influence on public education. A law that makes good people bad and bad people worse is a bad law.

Many of us believe that the greatest fault in NCLB (and in the current reform movement generally) is that it misconstrues the aims of education and indeed misunderstands the very nature of education—especially education in a liberal democracy. The bedrock concept of liberal democracy is choice (or freedom). A system of schooling that provides few choices and fails to prepare its students to make well-informed choices in the future does not deserve the label *education*, and it undermines the liberal democracy it should support. With an appropriate understanding of equality, standards, and testing, we should be prepared to argue that schools should be offering more, not fewer, choices on courses, projects, learning objectives, and modes of evaluation. In the chapter on choice, I will make this argument and suggest ways in which schools might better help students to prepare for life in a liberal democracy.

Some time ago, I visited a school in southern California. Because of my own background as a secondary school mathematics teacher, I naturally gravitated to the math department. One math teacher complained about the new block schedule under which the school was working. It might be fine for other subjects, she said, but it was no good for math. The conversation went like this:

NEL: Why are you doing it?

TEACHER: Well, you know, we're in the middle of school reform.

NEL (pretending ignorance): Oh? Reform, eh? What was wrong?

TEACHER (baffled): What? I don't know that anything was wrong. Well, probably. Well, you know, reform—everyone is doing it all over the country.

NEL: Ah. But how was this particular tactic [block scheduling] chosen?

TEACHER (relieved): Oh, that's easy. We have an administrator who is quite a good grant writer, and there happened to be state money available for this innovation.

NEL: So in a sense, the solution [block scheduling] preceded identification of the problem.

TEACHER: Hmm. Yes, it looks that way.

In Chapter 1, we will examine the idea of reform. Can there be reform without the identification of a problem? Must we not ask what is wrong? If a problem is identified in one demographic area or one facet of schooling, should a proposed solution be imposed on all schools? Where should reform begin? Should reform proceed without reviewing the aims to which we are committed in education? Suppose a solution threatens the achievement of an important aim?

That chapter will be followed by a brief chapter devoted to the analysis of words and how their use or misuse can clarify or obfuscate the problems we see and strive to solve. Then we should be in a position to examine equality, accountability, standards, testing, and choice in the next few chapters. We will conclude with a consideration of what is at stake for our children, schools, and democracy and some suggestions for fresh thinking.

1

SCHOOL REFORM

T HIS CHAPTER is not intended as a history of school reform in America. I am interested, rather, in what motivates reform efforts, the questions that should be asked before reform is attempted, the likely consequences that should be anticipated, and the lessons to be learned from past efforts at reform. I am interested particularly in the current school reform dictated by NCLB and whether it will improve or harm our system of public education.

Although the word *reform* is often used to label any changes in schooling, such as the addition of kindergarten or manual training, in this book it will refer to attempts to make large changes in American schooling—changes that affect the entire K–12 system, especially in curriculum and classroom practices. Certainly, the present movement, largely under the control of NCLB, qualifies as a reform movement. Every grade and every classroom is affected by the establishment of standards and the required use of standardized testing to measure the performance of students and teachers. We can learn something about the kind of questions we should ask by looking at two past reform movements, and then turning to today's movement and NCLB.

THE FIRST REFORM MOVEMENT

Perhaps the largest and most significant reform movement ever attempted came about in the early 20th century. This was the movement that expanded the high school curriculum and established the comprehensive high school and its variety of differentiated courses and tracks. The era in which this movement occurred is often referred to as the Progressive Era, but it is important not to confuse this use of *progressive* with one more narrowly used to describe the educational thought of John Dewey and his followers. *Progressive* in the larger sense points to a whole constellation of groups and programs whose purpose was to redesign schools to fit a new age of industrialization and efficiency.

Many factors contributed to the growth of the comprehensive high school, prominent among them population growth, a huge influx of immigrants, industrialization, and urbanization. Since many young adolescents would no longer be employed at home on family farms and were yet too immature to work daily with machinery in factories, it made sense to keep them in school longer. Then, too, there were thousands of immigrants who were thought to need education in citizenship if they were to become loyal Americans. The new high school with its differentiated courses—preparing some young people for college and others for the industrial workforce—was identified as the institution to accomplish these purposes.

At the same time, some educational thinkers wanted to humanize the whole system. If not all high school graduates were preparing for college, then surely the curriculum should include problems of everyday living. But, if some students were to participate in new, expanded curricula, perhaps all students would profit from schooling guided by broader aims of education. In 1918, the *Cardinal Principles Report* reversed the long-influential "academics for all" ideas that had been set forth in the 1893 Committee of Ten report. Instead of a traditional academic curriculum for all students, the Cardinal Principles embraced broader aims for schools: health, command of the fundamental processes, worthy home-membership, vocation, citizenship, worthy use of leisure, and ethical character. How closely schools attempted to follow these aims over the next few decades is still widely debated. But it is clear that, whether or not they were followed in detail, the Cardinal Principles represented a new era in American schooling. Was the result a more generous, humane form of schooling, or was it one that deprived students of a rigorous education? Did it initiate pernicious comparisons and treatment of students thought to have widely different abilities?

There is no question that with the advent of differentiated courses and tracks, high school enrollment and graduation rates soared. In 1900, only about 7% of the U.S. population graduated from high school; by 1940, more than 70% of teenagers (ages 14–17) were enrolled in high school, and the graduation rate was over 50%. This was a truly astonishing accomplishment, and it set a precedent for education throughout the Western world. Critics of differentiated courses sometimes overlook this positive result as they deplore the loss of rigor in the new schools.

Reasonable people, even those enthusiastic about the new education, have to admit that the promise of a more humane, relevant curriculum was sometimes lost in a welter of courses that did not meet a standard of excellence. However, this failure does not suggest that differentiated courses should be abandoned. Rather, it suggests that all courses should be strengthened to meet new standards appropriate to broadened aims. The new curriculum offerings *were* more generous in that both traditional and new, non–college preparatory courses were offered. Traditional courses did not disappear; they were simply not required of everyone. There was, in principle and often in practice, something for everyone.

The most regrettable result of differentiated courses was the establishment of a hierarchy of tracks and assignment of students to those tracks on the basis of students' perceived abilities. Those deemed capable of college work were placed in the "highest" (i.e., the academic) track. Others were placed in commercial, industrial, or general tracks. The system was unquestionably pernicious in placing poor and minority students in "lower" tracks and undeniably irresponsible in often failing to provide strong courses in these tracks. It is not surprising that thoughtful educators and policymakers eventually rebelled and demanded an end to tracking. A major element in the current reform movement requires academic courses for all students. I will argue that this is a grave error, perhaps even a disastrous one. For now, let's simply record the issue and schedule it for later discussion.

The assignment of students to tracks on the basis of test scores and past school performance should have been questioned. We would be rightly ashamed today to use the sort of language employed earlier in labeling youngsters and consigning them to occupational destinies. The fundamental concept of liberal democracy is choice, or freedom to make significant choices, and democratic schools have the responsibility to prepare young people to make well-informed choices. The practice of offering differentiated tracks might be defended if (1) every track were to offer rich, relevant courses, and (2) students were allowed, with appropriate guidance, to make their own choice of track. Notice that if we take seriously the responsibility to help students make well-informed choices, we would question both the dictatorial assignment of students to particular tracks *and* the elimination of all choice by providing only one set of courses.

A sober review of the great progressive reform has to conclude that (1) it succeeded in making it possible for the majority of young people to enroll in and graduate from high school; (2) it maintained most of the traditional course of study while adding a great variety of courses (some of questionable value); and (3) it invented and supported a system of pernicious tracking. In light of these results, we should ask whether it is possible to strengthen the courses that have been properly criticized and, again, whether it is possible to reinvigorate a system of tracking that will eliminate the harmful, discriminatory practices of the past. It is not denied that the comprehensive high school reform went wrong, but I will argue that its faults can be remedied.

A SECOND REFORM MOVEMENT

Now, searching for basic questions, let's look at another large reform movement. After the launching of the Russian satellite Sputnik, in 1957, a near panic seized U.S. policymakers, who feared that the Russians had surpassed, or were about to surpass, American technology. Much of the blame for the country's perceived failure was placed on education, and the schools experienced a wave of curriculum reform, especially (although not only) in mathematics and science.

I was a high school math teacher in the 1960s, and to me, the new curricula were wonderful. Such excitement! Our medium-size school managed to offer the usual algebra, geometry, trigonometry sequence, plus calculus, probability and statistics, Hilbert geometry, and even abstract algebra. But most of the kids did not appreciate the New Math, and most of our teachers were bewildered by it. Some mathematicians and scientists also objected to the New Math, declaring that so far from advancing our technological expertise, it would weaken us further. Then, as it turned out, the Russians were not, after all, in a position to bury us scientifically or economically, and it seemed wrong to put so much emphasis on courses enjoyed by a relative few.

There are several lessons we should have learned from that attempt at widespread reform. First, questions should always be raised when critics try to tie economic or technological slumps to a failure of the schools. The connection is not at all clear, and those who make it should be forced to provide evidence for the possible links. The industrial growth and productivity of the United States in the 20th century was, by any measure, an extraordinary phenomenon. Should the schools be credited with this great success? Why not?

Second, we should perhaps be wary of turning curriculum decisions over entirely to subject matter experts. Certainly, they should play an advisory role in constructing school curricula, but this role should be limited. After all, most students are not going to become professional mathematicians or scientists, and many of the topics suggested by experts are of little interest or use to most citizens. A more reasonable approach is to maintain a continuous dialogue on the aims of education and collaborative study of what should be meant by the "fundamental processes" named in the *Cardinal Principles Report.*

Third, there is a positive lesson to be learned from the New Math era—that with financial support, educators and subject matter experts can produce creative, rigorous, and wonderfully varied curricula that appeal to our brightest students and teachers. I have several shelves full of texts created during this period of curriculum reform (largely in the 1960s), and there is nothing today to compare with their bold vision and creative presentation. But to use this lesson wisely, we have to be willing to provide different materials for students with different purposes and interests. Improved curricula for the mathematically talented and interested should properly be very different from equally strong curricula designed to help students master fundamental processes.

TODAY'S REFORM MOVEMENT

The reform movement that started roughly in 1983 with the publication of *A Nation at Risk* was, once again, motivated by concerns over the national economy. One paragraph from that report reads:

> If an unfriendly foreign power had attempted to impose on America the mediocre educational performance that exists today, we might well have viewed it as an act of war. As it stands, we have allowed this to happen to ourselves. We have even squandered the gains in student achievement made in the wake of the Sputnik challenge. Moreover, we have dismantled essential support systems which helped make those gains possible. We have, in effect, been committing an act of unthinking, unilateral educational disarmament. (National Commission on Excellence in Education, 1984, p. 5)

I'll return to this paragraph in the next chapter in a discussion of the power of language, but here it is enough to notice the language of threat and war. Observe also the reference to gains made after Sputnik. What sort of gains were these? As we saw in my brief summary, these gains were largely confined to a relatively small segment of the school population. How were they "squandered"? What "essential support systems" were dismantled?

There is no consideration in *A Nation at Risk* of the difficulties students had with the 1960s curriculum, nor do its recommendations even mention them. There is no mention, either, of the National Science Foundation (NSF) fellowships that provided essential support for teachers preparing to teach the new math and science courses. We may suppose that the NSF program was part of the support system that was dismantled, but the report does not suggest offering another such program. Moreover, reading the report carefully, one is surprised to find that the recommendations do not really follow logically from the findings in the commissioned papers. Indeed, some of the papers had good things to say about the curriculum and structure of American education; no comment is made on any of these positive points.

What, then, induced the commission to speak in terms of "an act of war"? Why did the report call for a complete overhaul of the American high school? The indicators of risk included "consistent declines" in scores on College Board achievement tests, decline in the SAT scores, and an increase in remedial mathematics courses in 4-year colleges. But nowhere do the authors discuss—or even mention—the great increase in the number of students taking SATs, graduating from high school, and going to college. With a substantial change in the test-taking population, we would expect a change in norms.

A Nation at Risk did claim one troubling (if true) finding—a drop in the actual number of students scoring at the very highest levels of the SATs. If this is a fact, it should cause us to think anew along the lines already indicated—different curricula for different aptitudes and interests.

NO CHILD LEFT BEHIND

Most readers are likely to be familiar with the main points of NCLB. I'll review them briefly here.

The law requires that all students be proficient in mathematics and reading (language arts) by 2014. It leaves up to each state the choice of tests and the scores that will count as proficient. The variation in state proficiency levels is already generating controversy, and there is some agitation for a national curriculum and national standards.

Under NCLB, students must be tested in math and reading annually through grades 3–8 and at least once in high school. They must also be tested in science at three grade levels.

Every school is expected to make adequate yearly progress (AYP) along trajectory lines starting in 2001–02 and reaching 100% proficiency in 2013–14. Again, the states establish these lines, and many states have drawn broken lines that require relatively little progress in the first 5 years and thus very steep progress in later years. One cannot but suppose that these states are avoiding for the present the penalties that accompany failing to make AYP, hoping that things will change before they are called upon to do the impossible.

Data reporting student progress must be disaggregated, and every group must make AYP if a school is to be credited with doing so. All students, limited-English-proficient (LEP) students, educationally disadvantaged students (those in special education), and students in every major racial/ethnic category must meet the criterion for AYP. There have been some changes in the demands for the proficiency of LEP and special education students, and it is predictable that further changes will be required.

There are serious penalties for failing to make AYP: After 2 years of failure, schools must adopt an improvement plan and notify parents that they may transfer their children to nonfailing schools. After 3 years, the improvement plan must be continued, and parents may obtain supplementary tutoring from private educational providers at the expense of the district. After 4 years, serious changes must be made, for example, new curricula, changes in school personnel, and extension of the school day or year. After 5 years, schools are subject to complete restructuring and may be managed by a private firm under contract with the state.

In addition, the law requires that all classes be taught by "fully qualified" teachers. The determination of what is meant by *fully qualified* is left to the states. At present, it usually means credentialed. School districts are required to inform parents if their children are taught by "unqualified" teachers. Perversely, the private tutors hired by a school district need not be "qualified."

This is a brief introduction to the main points of NCLB. It is a cumbersome law—almost 1,000 pages in length. We could challenge its many requirements from both practical and logical viewpoints, but we'll defer that task until later. As we move through the coming chapters, we will revisit some of these requirements, but this short sketch may be sufficient to get us started. At present, we are interested in the broader topic of school reform movements, what triggers them, and what might predict their success or failure.

EDUCATIONAL AND PHILOSOPHICAL DIFFERENCES

Throughout the past century, philosophical differences have existed in educational thought. These differences are often blamed, by the people on opposing sides, for the perceived failings of our schools. Even before the Sputnik panic, critics were outraged by what they saw as deterioration in the high school curriculum. Arthur Bestor, for example, attacked everything associated with differentiated courses and tracks, especially curricula identified with Deweyan progressivism. We know that Dewey and his colleagues, representing variously the child-centered approach, social reconstruction, life adjustment, and the project method, were influential in educational theory, but historians tell us that we simply cannot assess their influence on actual practice. Indeed, the concrete evidence we do have suggests strongly that students from genuinely progressive high schools performed well academically.

In the 1970s, the shoe was—briefly—on the other foot; traditionalists were under attack, and advocates of more progressive approaches expressed outrage over the "mindlessness" rampant in our schools. This was the heyday for open education, store-front schools, integration, decentralization, and community control. But it was also an era torn by struggles over civil rights, the antiwar movement, and crowding of our colleges with young men desperate to avoid service in Vietnam.

My main point here is a controversial one—that differences in educational philosophy have had relatively little effect on American schools. Social and economic events have had far greater effects. The press of population growth, immigration, and industrialization fueled the movement toward comprehensive high schools in the early 20th century, and after that, occasional worries about the nation's economic or technological supremacy triggered attempts at reform. (The huge effort on behalf of racial integration triggered by the 1954 *Brown* decision caused an upheaval in school arrangements, but not in curriculum; it does not qualify as a reform movement in the sense we are addressing here.) Sometimes, however, a confluence of forces and a conglomeration of interests come together to favor a particular approach to schooling. At the beginning of the 21st century, we live in such a time. It seems now that differences in educational philosophy are critical, but almost certainly other factors are operating. What is driving the present reform movement?

A CLOSER LOOK AT RECENT REFORM

Today's reform movement is typical in that it began with alarmist language from critics. *A Nation at Risk* appeared at a time of economic recession and, like earlier critical reports, it blamed the schools for the predicted loss of competitiveness. With hindsight, it is easy to see that the report exaggerated the failure of our schools and played upon our economic fears. Just a few years later, the nation entered a decade of unprecedented prosperity. Were the schools responsible for this success? No one suggested such a possibility.

Why, then, didn't the movement generated by *A Nation at Risk* fall apart, as so many other attempts at reform have done? (Of course, it still might fall apart, but it appears in 2007 to be growing, not collapsing.) There was nothing in the larger society comparable to the sweeping changes that supported the great reform of the early 20th century.

We can't answer this difficult question with certainty, but I'll suggest some powerful possibilities. Perhaps the most powerful: Earlier reform movements were not backed by the federal government. The first Elementary and Secondary Education Act (1965) was not embraced with universal enthusiasm, and well into the 1970s, strong critics opposed attempts by the federal government to finance—never mind mandate—new curricula. Second, social reaction to the student rebellions during the Vietnam War favored more conservative forms of schooling ("back to basics"), and the flurry of excitement surrounding open education was short lived. For conservatives, it was a matter of eliminating the Department of Education, or working within it to change the shape of education. With gradual, if reluctant, acceptance of a role for the federal government in K–12 schooling, the stage was set for changes directed by those in federal positions.

A third powerful factor can be found in the nation's unresolved problems of race and poverty. It has long been clear that poor and minority children have often been ill-served by our public schools. The achievement gap between Blacks/Hispanics and Whites was cited explicitly as a reason for passing the No Child Left Behind Act. Certainly, most of us agree that something should be done to improve the educational and life chances of Black and Hispanic children.

But there are at least two reasons to doubt the wisdom of trying to make things right through NCLB. First, the problems experienced by many minority children are not confined to schooling. Children who live in substandard housing, have no health insurance, live with an overworked single parent, have a parent in prison, and may be periodically homeless or in state custody can hardly be expected to do well in school. Instead of pointing an accusing finger at educators and insisting, "No excuses," policymakers would do well to look at the conditions named as "excuses" and do something about them. The suspicion arises that the tremendous emphasis on schools and achievement tests may be a smoke screen of sorts—a fine-sounding effort to distract the voting public from real, pressing social problems.

A second reason to doubt the sincerity of those who concentrate on the achievement gap is found in the nature of the proposed solution. As I pointed out earlier, we have known for years that many of our urban schools need a complete overhaul. If the main problems are located in urban schools, why would sensible people devise and impose a massive plan of reform on *all* schools? The waste involved in such a move is likely to be enormous, and it may well leave the real problem almost untouched.

Many of us believe that NCLB embodies a major error. If policymakers are serious about improving the lot of poor and minority children, they should address the constellation of problems faced by those youngsters. We could, for example, launch a sort of educational Manhattan Project to study the problems and create better schools. If, instead, policymakers shift their argument and fall back on the language of 1983, claiming that, in general, "our schools are failing," they have to provide convincing evidence that this is so. There are reasons for doubting that this evidence can be produced. As a result of mistaken efforts, the very children who are the ostensible targets of educational reform may be further hurt.

We will return to the problem of minorities and urban schools in Chapter 3, in a discussion of "solutions" that prescribe the same curriculum for all. One lesson we should have learned from previous attempts at school reform is that uniformity of curriculum and instruction is almost certainly a mistake; no one is well served by such plans. We should note, also, that some powerful thinkers are now suggesting a new conception of universal education. The new concept moves away from discipline-oriented curriculum toward a problem and theme organization that emphasizes values, attitudes, flexibility, working in teams, and critical thinking rather than subject matter information. This is an important idea, and I'll say more about it later. If it is the wave of the future, as some thinkers suggest, we are actually moving backward in our current attempts to standardize and test subject matter knowledge.

We should also have learned that the connection between academic achievement in our K–12 schools and the capacity of our nation to compete economically is questionable. In a century marked by educational differentiation, the United States established an astonishing record of invention, industrial productivity, military dominance, and knowledge production, and the system allowed most young people to graduate from high school. That record is not a failing one.

Another factor that may support today's efforts at reform is the growth of larger schools. After the Sputnik launch, schools in the United States, especially high schools, became much larger. In part, that growth was necessitated by the press of increasing population, but it was also a result of deliberate thinking. Some educators believed that small schools could not offer the special courses in science and advanced mathematics that the nation now required. This claim, it turns out, could have been challenged. Small schools can and often do provide advanced science and math. Moreover, as mentioned earlier, we should have raised serious questions about the variety and quality of courses to be provided for very different populations. We should have questioned both the claim about small schools and the basic premise of the need for more math and science for everyone.

But we now have large schools. One effect is that parents no longer feel that they know what is going on in these schools. The fact that discipline and security problems have increased lends credibility to the possibility that achievement, too, has deteriorated. There is a nervous sense that things are out of control and that everything—attendance, conduct, achievement—should come under a form of standardization. Even parents who are satisfied with their own local schools tend to believe that schools in general are in a mess.

One last factor to be mentioned here is the influence of business on schools. Business forces have always affected our schools, and periodically suggestions have been made that schools should be run more like businesses. That idea has recently grown more powerful, in part because of the increase in school size. As we will see, the language of accountability came to education directly from the business world. What made it so attractive? Were the schools, in fact, not accountable?

Although the business community has always exerted some influence on schools, its interest has increased greatly in the last decade. Some of this interest comes from the needs of employers for workers with adequate skills, but many studies have shown that on-the-job skill training is more powerful than most of that provided by schools. Moreover, if the thinkers who now recommend new forms of universal education are right in emphasizing values, attitudes, work habits, flexibility, and critical thinking, then business's push for more subject matter knowledge is a mistake.

Some business interest is civically inspired, benign, even supportive. But much of it is motivated by self-interest. Schools represent a large audience for consumer products, and discontent with public schools opens the possibility of a whole new market for private (for-profit) schools. We need not impugn the motives of today's reformers to acknowledge that many entrepreneurial types see schooling as a huge, relatively untapped market. Moreover, the testing industry is booming, and the supplementary tutoring assured by NCLB is already worth billions. It would be a mistake to overlook the interest of business in the current reform.

Several factors, then, account for the persistence, even growth, of the present reform movement. I have pointed to the enlarged role of the federal government, an increase in the number of larger schools, the influence of business, and recognition of the continuing achievement gap. All of these factors are, however, bound up in another powerful phenomenon—the use of language to distract, dissemble, and persuade. We turn to that issue next.

2

WORDS

H UMAN BEINGS use words to communicate. Through words, we pass information to others, express our needs and feelings, ask questions, and give directions and explanations. Our speech can be clear or abstruse, emotionally charged or neutral, honest or dishonest, succinct or wordy, relevant to present concerns or off the point. In everyday communication, we appreciate—sometimes even demand—clarity, honesty, relevance, and emotionally appropriate language. But in political situations, we often accept language that is cliché ridden and may not express the real motives of its speakers. We need to question such language.

LANGUAGE TO DISSEMBLE

George Orwell's *1984* provided us with the 20th century's classic work on language used to dissemble. Newspeak, the language under development in Orwell's horrifying totalitarian state, was designed to diminish, not extend, meaning. In Newspeak, meaning is severely limited. Communication cannot be used for analysis or to express critical thinking. It is ideally designed to show conformity and to make doublethink sound reasonable.

Doublethink (it was Orwell who coined the now common term) refers to the acceptance of two contradictory statements as simultaneously true. Many of us are guilty of doublethink in certain areas of our lives. For example, it is not unusual for people to believe at one and the same time that God is in control of everything and, yet that luck will determine the next event. In Orwell's Oceania, people were expected to believe that "war is peace," "freedom is slavery," and "ignorance is strength."

Religious language is highly susceptible to doublethink, and some philosophers charge that people are often unwilling to discuss religion in open public arenas precisely because genuine discussion might trigger critical thinking, which in turn might well uncover instances of doublethink. Some of the greatest works in religious philosophy—Spinoza's comes to mind—have been attempts to rid theological language of doublethink. Typically, these attempts are not widely appreciated, and efforts are made to suppress discussion.

Today, many careful thinkers refer to the "Clean Air Initiative" and "Healthy Forests Reforestation Act" as examples of Newspeak operating in our own society. These critics point out that the acts in question permit the opposite of what is promised in the words that name them. Under the Clean Air Initiative, more air pollution is allowed; under the Healthy Forests Reforestation Act, more forests can be destroyed. If the critics are right, the words used to label these acts convey the opposite of what is intended. The power of such language is recognized by critics of the No Child Left Behind Act. Seeking to show that the name of the act is intended to dissemble, one critical book is entitled *Many Children Left Behind*.

Another way to mislead without dissembling outright is to borrow language from one domain and transfer it intact to another. As I pointed out earlier, much of the language in *A Nation at Risk* is alarmist; it uses words such as *war, foreign power*, and *unilateral disarmament*. Readers who might otherwise look for carefully presented evidence may be swept into premature agreement by language that induces fear. When policymakers warn that the United States will lose its competitive edge, that other nations are producing more engineers than the United States, and that our students lag dangerously behind those of other nations, audiences rarely ask for evidence to support the warnings. They are moved by emotion. Fairminded writers would at least inform their readers that these claims are disputed. For example, it has been claimed by other responsible observers that the nation's economic health has little to do with student test scores, and some nations whose students score well on tests produce relatively few innovations (several Asian countries have expressed concern about the apparent lack of creativity in their students). It has also been argued that the United States still produces the greatest number of engineers per capita. And if population differences, socioeconomic status within the country, age, and school retention are taken into account, U.S. students are not doing badly. Who is right? My purpose is not to argue one side or the other on these issues but to point out that emotion-laden language is likely to swamp carefully researched, calmly reported conclusions.

Education today is laden with language borrowed from the business world. The language of "zero tolerance" rules came directly from "zero defects" in manufacturing. Careful analysis should have resulted in caution. School communities might well adopt zero tolerance attitudes ("we do not tolerate violence") without establishing zero tolerance rules. Acting on these rules often makes school people look foolish, as though they are incapable of making sound judgments. "Accountability"—an idea we will examine in some depth—also came from business. Before institutionalizing it, we should have asked what it might mean in education, and whether we might do better with a word more appropriate to schooling. Similarly, much of our language on leadership has been borrowed from business, and many policymakers assume a complete set of generic characteristics for leadership, whereas some of the most important characteristics may be domain specific. Even the word *equality*, borrowed from the domain of politics, takes on strange connotations in education. We must attempt to analyze these borrowings.

We should be careful, however, in our analysis of cases of doublethink. The fact that the language dissembles does not imply with certainty that the writer or speaker intends to dissemble. There are critics today who claim that the designers and advocates of NCLB intend to weaken the public schools and thus pave the way for privatization. There are even those who suspect that the intention—far from leaving no child behind—is to leave many children behind, thus ensuring a cadre of poorly educated people to staff the booming service industry. They may be right. But we need not attribute questionable motives to the people promoting NCLB. The language itself dissembles, and those supporting it may be guilty only of doublethink—believing that children are being helped when much evidence and clear logic suggests they are being hurt. We'll consider other examples of doublethink in each of the following chapters.

There are times when it is hard to avoid skepticism about motives, and we should be frank when these moments occur. For example, most policymakers are insistent on "evidence-based research" and "evidence-based practice," but many of them ignore research that offers solid evidence when that evidence points in a direction other than the one they have chosen. A prominent example of this tactic is the continuing practice of retaining students in grade when they fail a high-stakes test—even though research shows convincingly that retention almost always makes the student's performance worse, not better.

Orwell also warned us about the dissembling power of acronyms. Acronyms save space and needless repetition of words; within an article, they can be effective. Even the most prestigious publications today use them profusely. But careful readers find themselves returning again and again to the original definition so that they can be sure of what they are reading. The full name of an agency, law, or strategy may arouse concern, but the concern fades away with the acronym. The familiar SAT, for example, once stood for Scholastic Aptitude Test, but doubts were raised about the test's validity in measuring aptitude. Then, briefly, it became the Scholastic Assessment Test, but this label seemed odd—rather like saying Scholastic Test Test, as Alfie Kohn has remarked. Now the SAT is just the SAT, and many educators (not all, happily) have given up asking what it measures. It is simply a test that college applicants must take; it is important and may determine students' academic future. We will encounter other cases of meaning lost by way of acronym.

As we move through an analysis of the reform movement directed by NCLB, we will be reminded repeatedly of how language can dissemble, intentionally or through doublethink: by labeling that conveys the opposite of what is intended or of the actual result, by borrowing language from another domain without analyzing it, by the use of emotion-laden words, and by the use of acronyms.

POLITICAL CORRECTNESS

Some people are highly critical of "political correctness"—the practice of monitoring language to remove words or phrases that give offense to various religious, gender, or ethnic groups. They feel that the movement has gone too far, and has had the effect of eliminating conversations that may be essential to democratic life. Diane Ravitch has argued persuasively that school textbooks have eliminated much controversial material, and thereby weakened the curriculum. I think she is right on this.

But political correctness is not all bad. In a conversation a few years ago at Stanford, a colleague staunchly defended the practice of censuring some language. "These guys," she said, "are mad because they can't shoot off their nasty mouths any more." She had a good point. If by *political correctness* we mean insistence on the use of language that does not use racial, religious, ethnic, or gender epithets, the practice is to be commended. We should be politically correct.

However, political correctness carried beyond the proscription of such epithets runs perilously close to Newspeak. It not only forbids the use of certain words, but it also restricts the range of topics to be discussed and even cuts off critical thinking. Not long ago, the former president of Harvard, Lawrence Summers, ignited a verbal firestorm when he suggested at a public meeting that the absence of women in science and mathematics at the university might be explained by genetic factors. Most of us might agree that (1) Summers' statement was undiplomatic and, obviously, politically incorrect, and (2) there exist more likely hypotheses to explain the phenomenon. However, his hypothesis might still be right; it is a semiopen question in science. Could the idea have been expressed in such a way that reasoned debate might have followed? Or has it become impossible to discuss such matters even in academic settings?

Consider another example. Several researchers have found that parent–child dialogue differs greatly across socioeconomic groups. In general, middle- and upper-class dialogue is rich in both concepts and information, whereas working-class parent–child communication tends to be short and often restricted to commands and compliments. If this finding is accurate, an important educational problem has been identified. Schools should give more attention to parenting and, particularly, to enriching parent–child dialogue. But some critical researchers have reacted to this research with outrage, claiming that it represents a much deplored deficit model. Because so many minority parents are situated in the lower economic group, the result is racially offensive. Still, the offending researchers may be right, and we should find a way to discuss the issue without insulting one another.

Some years ago, I wrote an article branding the variability hypothesis a "pernicious hypothesis." The variability hypothesis states that males vary more than females on intellectual traits; women are, in general, more alike. The hypothesis is pernicious because of its history and because of its use of male-biased traits to represent intellectual capacity. I would now add another criterion for calling it pernicious—confirmation or disconfirmation would be unlikely to improve the condition of either group. Such research only raises hackles. If I were writing the article today, I would acknowledge the propriety of continued research only if a researcher could suggest some socially worthwhile purpose for doing the research. A hypothesis that offends a particular group may be worth exploring if its confirmation or disconfirmation might lead to improvement of that group's condition.

Political correctness sometimes weakens the school curriculum by eliminating the discussion of controversial issues. It seems right, for example, to reject the statement, "Columbus discovered America," because native people were already living on the continent. But that recognition does not demand the omission of all discussion of Columbus's achievement; both positive and negative results following his discovery should be discussed. He did, after all, discover America for the Western world. The idea is to present all reasonable sides of every issue as fairly as possible and, especially, to promote a continuing discussion of what is reasonable. There are scholars who believe that schools have gone too far with the inclusion of material critical of the United States and its institutions, and there are opposing scholars who believe the schools have not gone nearly far enough. Both sides should be heard, and students should be encouraged to explore the dangers of ultranationalistic pride on the one hand and a cynical lack of patriotism on the other.

Political correctness can also weaken or distort international diplomacy. Recently, a few writers in both the United States and Israel have begun to draw our attention to the lack of constructive dialogue on Israel's mistakes and mistreatment of the Palestinians. The dialogue has been hampered, these writers claim, by fears of being perceived as anti-Semitic. But clearly, if the conduct of Israel and the United States on Israel's behalf could be improved by critical discussion, we are remiss in neglecting it.

An education worthy of the label *education* should promote open discussion of controversial issues and language, insisting only that speakers respect their listeners and refrain from language that insults or demeans anyone (Noddings, 2006). To ask, "What do you mean by that?" is a sign of respect. To suggest that an offensive statement might still contain a nucleus of truth is a mark of scholarly wisdom. Then the question becomes one of showing how the issue under contention can be pursued without offense. One of the greatest defects in the system guided by NCLB is the erosion of intellectual habits of mind. We are living in a new age of self-righteous anti-intellectualism.

THE LANGUAGE OF REFORM

The language of current reform, No Child Left Behind, is hard to oppose, but we should ask, What do you mean by that? It is clear that NCLB does not mean to reject the policy of leaving kids behind in the old-fashioned sense of retaining them in grade. To the contrary, the high-stakes testing accompanying NCLB has resulted in many children being retained in grade. One can argue plausibly that students should not be expected to move on to work that requires a foundation they have not yet established, but there are ways of providing for differing rates of progress that do not involve the emotionally devastating impact of being held back in grade. People who are genuinely concerned about the well-being of children should consider how a fourth grader feels when he or she is left back, and the evidence is clear that retention usually retards educational performance instead of improving it. Moreover, if we were seriously interested in helping each child to move along from a firm foundation of established knowledge and skills, we would not demand that all students —regardless of preparation—take and pass the same tests. There is a fundamental contradiction in this practice.

Advocates of NCLB might mean that we should not judge what a child is capable of doing on the basis of factors such as race, sex, or socioeconomic status. We should affirm this commitment heartily. But notice that this does not commit us to the highly questionable proposition that all children can or should meet the same standards.

Perhaps *no child left behind* means that every child will have a fair opportunity to reap the economic rewards of higher education. That's what many people seem to have in mind, and many thoughtless speakers say right out that students who do not achieve a college education will be "doomed" to a mediocre—even impoverished—economic life. What can these people be thinking? If everyone goes to college, our society will still need service workers: people to grow, transport, cook, and serve food; make beds and clean rooms; sell retail goods; care for children; clean houses and offices; drive buses and taxis; clean and repair streets; maintain electric and telephone lines; deliver mail and all sorts of packages. The society will still need police, fire fighters, custodians, pet groomers, cleaners and tailors, truckers, gas station attendants, toll takers, mechanics, cashiers, hairdressers, barbers, carpenters, painters, plumbers, gardeners, ticket-takers, car salespersons, real estate agents, bank clerks, fishermen, butchers, produce handlers, and military personnel. Are all of these people doomed to near-impoverishment? Why? Are we willing to say that "we" gave them a fair chance to do better, and they simply did not take advantage of the opportunity? Education can lift individuals out of poverty; it cannot do the same for the entire society. Society at large must face its social and economic problems by ensuring that no person who works full time at an honest job lives in poverty. We are an interdependent society. If we accept this responsibility at the societal level, we should be prepared at the school level to reconsider what it means to educate—to devise an education that prepares students for a whole life, not simply an economic existence. There is more to education than preparation for economic life.

The current language of educational reform suggests that everyone should go to college and that all school children should meet the same standards at the same age. The slogan heard everywhere is, "All children can learn." Again, we should ask, What do you mean by that? *What* can all children learn? *Why* should they learn the material we suppose they can learn? It is just silly to say that all children can learn whatever the school prescribes. Anyone who has actually taught knows that this is untrue.

So the careful, generous educator settles down to ask exactly what it is that all children can and should learn. Probably, most children can learn to read but not at the same time or at the same depth. Thus we work patiently and diligently to be sure that all (or almost all) children acquire enough skill at reading to function adequately in a complex society. What does it mean "to function adequately"? We must keep this question open and, as we explore it, keep working with children, encouraging them, praising progress, assuring them that we are with them in the struggle to learn. We do not fail them, retain them, or remind them that they are in the bottom decile of some standardized test.

Instead of the sensible approach just sketched, too often we simply assert (with a goodly measure of self-righteousness) that all children can and should learn algebra. Because we know that, given variation in aptitude and interest, many children cannot learn what was once described as algebra, we place them all in a class called *algebra* and proceed to teach mathematical trivia. This is neither generous nor honest; it is pedagogical fraud. Students have *algebra* on their high school transcripts, but they know almost nothing of the subject, and if they go on to college, they need remedial mathematics. Or they may live in a city that requires some sort of state examination, and only a handful of the defrauded students pass it. Many high schools in our large cities are now experiencing this result.

Instead of shouting, "No excuses," at educators in such settings, we would do better to ask what these youngsters might profitably study. What mathematics is necessary for ordinary life in a liberal democratic society? What topics might appeal to them? How can we match a curriculum to their real talents and interests? When we insist that all children can and must learn academic mathematics, we hurt them doubly: They fail in subjects they have not chosen, and they are deprived of studies at which they might excel.

The insistence on academic coursework for all is often made in the name of equality. We turn to that topic next.

3

EQUALITY

W E ARE ALL familiar with the unambiguous use of *equality* in mathematics, although even in that field the concept is more sophisticated than most people realize. It is the use of *equality* as it is borrowed from the political domain that is of most interest to us here. When we speak of equality in the social/political domain, we refer to equality before the law and the equal rights of citizens to participate in political life—to vote, run for office, and speak their opinions. Beyond national citizenship, we speak of the dignity of human lives and the equal worth of each life.

In the domain of education, the notion of equality is usually found in discussions of equal opportunity, but this—like *equality* itself—is a complex idea. Today equal opportunity is often equated with equal results. Indeed, that idea is at the heart of NCLB's stated mission: There should be no substantial gap in achievement between Whites and any other racial/ethnic group. All groups should be equal in results as exhibited in achievement test scores. If we put aside groups of limited-English-proficient speakers and special education students, for whom the demand is logically ridiculous, we should be able to agree that substantial differences between, say, racial groups is an indication that something is wrong. Such differences should not exist. But the question remains: *What* is wrong? And can the schools be expected to identify and remedy the problem?

EQUALITY AS SAMENESS

Before addressing those questions, we should note that hardly anyone believes that all individual differences, as contrasted with group differences, can be removed. Yet the requirements of NCLB suggest that all students should experience the same curriculum and achieve roughly the same results. One troublesome effect of NCLB is that group and individual differences have been confounded. When we expect all children to master the same material, we may easily fall into this confusion. Which things should all students learn, and at what point should we provide different educational experiences for children with different aptitudes and interests? This is a question of fundamental importance in education, and the current standards movement has suppressed its discussion.

Let's pursue it for a bit. Early in the 20th century, Charles W. Eliot, who had ten years earlier insisted on a uniform classical education for all high school students, now recommended a differentiated curriculum:

> If democracy means to try to make all children equal or all men equal, it means to fight nature, and in that fight democracy is sure to be defeated. There is no such thing among men as equality of nature, of capacity for training, or of intellectual power. (1905, p. 13)

This is almost certainly right. Children are not equal in most capacities, and surely not in interests. Their educations, then, should differ. Plato, Rousseau, and Dewey all agreed on this. Indeed, we might argue that there is nothing so *unequal* in education as sameness. But it does not follow that school authorities should decide unilaterally what studies should be required of a particular student, and it does not mean that there are *no* competencies that should be expected of all students. These thorny issues are almost entirely neglected in the wake of NCLB. I'll return to them in the chapter on standards.

In an essay on equality and excellence, John W. Gardner (1961/1984) recognized the worth of all competent workers, and also recognized that some children who would one day be highly competent in, say, a trade might have great difficulty with academic studies. Still, he argued that all children should have a strong academic program, even if that meant that many would fail in school. His argument focused on the school's main purpose—academic learning. It was asking too much, he said, to expect the school to provide substantially different and yet uniformly high-quality programs to children with very different talents. He believed that youngsters who failed in school could be helped to understand that such failure was only one sort of failure and that they could still be successful in occupational life. I think this requires a level of heroism on the part of youngsters who fail in school. How can they understand that the failure they have experienced for their entire young lives is just one form of failure? The schools in a democratic society have to provide for individual differences.

Gardner regretted the effects on students who might struggle academically, but in the interests of excellence, he wanted to make the job of the schools manageable. Others have felt that one standard academic curriculum serves the best interest of both schools and students. Years ago, Robert Maynard Hutchins delivered an aphorism that has often been quoted: "The best education for the best is the best education for all." Years later, Mortimer Adler repeated it in an argument for democratic equality in schooling. Careful thinkers should challenge all three of the "bests" in Hutchins's aphorism. Who are the "best" for whom the "best" education was designed? Generally, the "best" were drawn from the economically well-to-do, with a few academically talented less well-off students invited to join the circle. We could spend many useful hours exploring and analyzing the curriculum that was constructed for this privileged group. Indeed, many thoughtful observers call it "privileged knowledge." What was it designed to do? Was it designed to increase democratic participation or to ensure that power was retained by the "best"? What exactly did it comprise? How much variation did it exhibit? We cannot launch the needed investigation here, but take note that such an investigation is needed. Adler was simply wrong when he claimed that the "shape of the best education for the best is not unknown to us" (1982, p. 7). Living in a world where the best and brightest have led us into war generation after generation, where corporate greed is once again rampant, where religion has not weeded out its fundamentalist irrationalities, where poverty persists in the midst of riches, and the earth itself suffers from human abuse, we can hardly claim to know the shape of the best education. On the contrary, we have only the barest outline, and it is a problem we should be working on diligently.

Surely the best education for the finest carpenters should differ in significant ways from the best education for the best nurses or teachers. If we share a Whitmanesque view of democracy, we would not talk about a "best" at all without appending a noun of reference (say, an occupation), and then we would study that occupation or activity carefully before announcing criteria for our judgment of best. That still leaves the problem of how to educate for citizenship, private life, moral life, spirituality. However, when we point to our own education and tell children that we will now generously insist that they be required to enjoy or endure that very same education, we convey an odd notion of equality. It amounts to saying that they can be equal if they are just like us. That is not a democratic approach. Of course, another way of looking at the problem is to say that even if people are not just like us, they deserve the same education but, as we saw, that position is hard to defend.

Some time ago, a neighbor, Joe, told me that he was a good citizen in high school during the early 1970s. In his sophomore year, he received an award for perfect attendance, but he had a difficult time with academic studies and did poorly on standardized tests. Fortunately, during his school years, those tests were not high stakes, and he graduated from high school. Joe had exceptional mechanical and artistic talents, but neither talent was recognized in high school; only his academic weaknesses were noted. However, Joe was encouraged by his family to get some post-secondary training in mechanics. Joe worked hard and made a decent living as a diesel mechanic, eventually owning his own small business. However, his high school years should have been both happier and more educational.

In Joe's story, we can see both success and failure. Schools in the 1960s and 1970s kept many students with nonacademic talents in school, but they rarely recognized or encouraged their talents. The comprehensive high school made it possible for Joe and kids like him to earn a diploma, but his nonacademic courses were poorly planned and executed, and Joe always felt like a second-class citizen. This pattern is one reason that thoughtful educators now reject tracking. Another reason, as we mentioned earlier, is that too many youngsters—often minorities—were arbitrarily assigned to nonacademic tracks. Neither of these reasons is in itself an argument against tracking; rather, they are both arguments against the ways in which tracking has been implemented.

Today boys like Joe often drop out of high school. Unable to compete with peers who are academically talented, uninterested in what is taught, and defeated by frequent failures on high-stakes tests, they simply give up. Without a high school diploma, they may wander from one unskilled job to another, on-and-off employment with few prospects. To make matters worse, such youngsters often avoid opportunities for any form of alternative training, fearing yet another failure.

School should be a place where talents are identified and encouraged. By forcing all students into the same curriculum, our society risks losing needed talents, and individuals may lose opportunities to find work at which they could be happy. Moreover, by expending excessive time and energy coercing reluctant students to learn material they hate, we neglect those who love the material and could move through it rapidly and in far greater depth.

I am arguing that tracking is not a bad idea, and I will say much more on how to implement a reasonable, democratic plan for tracking in the chapter on choice. Forcing everyone into the same curriculum is a bad idea. Sameness does not bring equality. On the contrary, sameness of studies aggravates inequality. Those who have the requisite aptitude and interest will (unless their progress is pedagogically impeded) pull far ahead of those whose aptitudes lie in a different domain.

There is another way in which the unexamined notion of equality may be leading us astray. Policymakers and educators today often claim that all high school graduates should be "ready for college or work," as though preparation for the two very different worlds should be identical. This is a controversial position, and readers should be aware that reasonable, responsible people differ on it. Recently, the ACT (American College Testing, Inc.) reported a study concluding that high school graduates needed roughly the same skills in communication and math for success in either college or midrange occupations. Note, however, that this does not permit us to conclude that the two groups need exactly the same courses to produce the requisite skills tested by ACT. A solid vocational course of study, one preparing students for postsecondary training, might produce the desired results. But readers should also be aware that the recommendations of ACT were not well supported by evidence and that many researchers have criticized them.

Supposing that preparation for work and preparation for college should be identical is a mistake with a long history rooted in a belief that the "best" education—loosely defined around theoretically oriented liberal arts—is the best preparation for all sorts of occupations. There are those today who want to differentiate sharply between traditional undergraduate degrees and those awarded to students preparing for a specific job. Indeed, the argument is made that the latter group should not receive degrees at all but, instead, some certificate that appropriately reflects their training. This attitude reminds us of the days in which liberally educated people objected to the presence of business and agriculture on university campuses. We have still not entirely overcome such prejudice.

I have no objection to specifying what a degree is "in"—that is, in what the student's preparation consists, but the idea that a general, theoretically oriented education prepares people better for all sorts of work than does training for a specific occupation is highly questionable. The most fundamental idea of genuine education is that it should lead students to seek further learning, and this can be accomplished through either general or specific programs of study at which students can achieve a measure of success. Moreover, the best practical programs may do a better job with theory than many theoretical programs that fail to make any connection to the practical. This is a point that John Dewey and, more recently, Mike Rose have made repeatedly. We will discuss later a new description of universal education that posits goals that can be pursued through either academic or vocational programs.

The last 2 years of high school might well be used to start some students on a training program that would lead to postsecondary training and work. Their success in such a program and the achievement of a high school diploma should encourage further study. True, such further study might not be of the academic sort usually associated with a traditional college education, but it should not be denigrated or thought of as second-class.

Recently, at an airport, I fell into conversation with a man who had just returned from a trip to Romania, where he had gone to recruit skilled machinists for his business. He had been unable to find qualified people in North America. There are still well-paying jobs that do not require a college education.

Do our high school students have reliable knowledge about where the jobs will be in the next decade, or are they beguiled by the notion that everyone who will amount to anything must go to college? Too often, students are told that everyone now needs academic knowledge because we are living in a postindustrial, information age. But they are rarely given the actual figures on where the most jobs will be found. (See the U.S. Bureau of Labor Statistics on this.) In the next decade, most job openings will be in the service sector. Of the ten jobs with the most openings, only one or two require a college education. The so-called knowledge world for which we try so hard to prepare all students has generated an enormous service world to support it. Already many college graduates are working at jobs that do not require a college education.

As we have seen, there are those who talk about equality but resist the "equalization" of postsecondary vocational courses and traditional programs. Why? Here, perhaps, we see the true colors of many who seem to espouse equality. One can endorse, as I do, an open recognition of difference and an honest disclosure of the content of all programs and still insist on an assessment of equal worth. Those who oppose the equalization of degrees offer equality through sameness: Study what I study, learn what I learn, and you will be equal to me.

It is true that, in general, over a lifetime, college graduates earn more than those with vocational training, but there are many exceptions, and in the past too many graduates of vocational programs fell into those programs by default, not by choice. They were considered not good enough for the more esteemed academic programs. If students were able to make such choices proudly, the picture might change. Sadly, some youngsters now reject postsecondary vocational education because they believe it might limit their chances. It might. But, on the other hand, it might open the door to a lifetime of vocational well-being. I am reminded here of the earlier study by Paul Willis that showed vividly how working-class boys resisted attempts to educate them academically, thereby ensuring that they would remain in the laboring class. Now young people, deprived of information on where most of the jobs will be, may decide—against their own interests—that they must undergo an academic education, even though a strong vocational education might suit them better.

The key seems to be thorough, patient, and respectful guidance. Students should be given the best possible information about programs and encouraged to study their own aptitudes and interests. Then they should be allowed to make their own choice of school program. Every program offered by our schools should be rich, relevant, and aimed at producing whole people as well as competent workers.

EQUAL OPPORTUNITY

Now we have to face the problem with which we started this chapter: How can we equalize educational achievement across racial and ethnic groups? This is one admirable goal of NCLB. While virtually all of us agree that individuals will continue to vary in aptitude and achievement, we see no obvious reason why the average achievement of racial or ethnic groups should differ significantly. But they do. Why?

It is reasonable to ask the "why" question before deciding on a definite and expensive answer to our first question. Advocates of NCLB seem to suppose that the main reason for the Black/White achievement gap is the low expectations teachers hold for Black students. They have a catchy phrase for this attitude—"the soft bigotry of low expectations." We have to acknowledge that some teachers may be guilty of this charge, but many are not. In any case, before imposing a set of threats, sanctions, and punishments on everyone, policymakers should have asked if a blame-and-punish approach is the best way to motivate people. I'll come back to this important question.

There are still a few people who answer the "why" question with a single word, *genetics*, and my guess is that there are others who agree with this answer but are constrained by political correctness not to admit it. Given the growing stack of scientific evidence that throws doubt on the concept of race itself, a hypothesis stating a genetic factor for academic inferiority cannot reasonably be regarded as an open scientific question. It has to be labeled a pernicious hypothesis because it inflicts great harm and holds no promise for social improvement. Yet it must be discussed—just as we must discuss the evolution/creationism debate. Neither the genetic explanation for academic inferiority nor the creationism hypothesis can be considered a viable scientific hypothesis, but people hold to each of them. How have these hypotheses been answered? Why should well-educated people reject them? In the case of the discredited genetic hypothesis, what are some powerful and more likely alternatives?

Social and economic alternatives should head the list. We have known at least since the Coleman reports in the late 1960s that school success is highly correlated with socioeconomic status and the educational status (or interest) of families. Since kids from middle-, upper-middle-, and upper-class families generally do better on achievement tests and in school work generally, it has been argued that one solution to the achievement gap would be to make everyone middle class. Impossible? Well, the Nordic nations have come close to realizing this ideal—to reducing poverty to small proportions. At the very least, addressing the problem of poverty and its attendant ills should be considered as one powerful (and perhaps morally obligatory) approach to reducing the achievement gap. And even if it failed to reduce the achievement gap, it would still be the right thing to do.

This approach also offers an argument for affirmative action, even affirmative action that risks a blow to meritocratic selection procedures. As Isaiah Berlin wisely pointed out, we cannot always act upon all of our values simultaneously. Sometimes, cautiously and with some regret, we have to sacrifice one value to realize another. If vigorous implementation of affirmative action might reduce the achievement gap, it seems worth trying. As the young people who benefit from affirmative action move upward on the socioeconomic scale, their children stand an even better chance of achieving success in school.

But what of the evidence suggesting that a Black/White gap remains even within a given socioeconomic group? That is troublesome indeed. However, we must face realistically the possibility that it may take several generations for the economic effects of affirmative action to be completely realized in the school success of children. At the same time, we must minimize the trauma suffered by youngsters whose dreams are somewhat dampened by our social commitment. Highly qualified Whites who are displaced at an elite school by less qualified Blacks will almost surely find a place at some accredited institution. The suffering must be acknowledged but not exaggerated. It should be pointed out, too, that many Black students also suffer; they are thought to be recipients of special treatment even when they are not. So the solution is far from perfect. Should it be tried?

While we look at the problem of poverty, we must also consider other explanations for the achievement gap. The effect of stereotypes must be explored. Claude Steele has shown persuasively that "stereotype threat" can be enormously damaging. If students are told that people like them do not do well on certain tests or tasks, the chances increase that, in fact, they will not do well. Something like this may be operating also with women and mathematics. Often told that women lag behind men in mathematics—that women are just "not up to it"—most women do indeed lag behind men. Young Blacks are doubly intimidated—first by remarks from the White community about their general academic ability and, second, by members of the Black community who accuse them of "acting White" when they apply themselves to school work.

Another question implicit in this discussion is what it means to be qualified and how achievement should be measured. It is a fundamental question to be addressed in the chapters on accountability, standards, and testing. We should remind students that they should not consider themselves academically better or worse than others merely on the basis of test scores.

Similarly, we can ask questions about what it means to have an "equal opportunity." Must it mean an equal opportunity to go to college? Might it be better construed as an equal opportunity to develop one's own talents?

A few months ago, the *New York Times* ran a series of articles on the near-epidemic of diabetes in the Bronx. A 15-year-old Hispanic girl, recently diagnosed with diabetes, was interviewed. She knew almost nothing about the disease, comparing it with "a cold," and she was not at all worried about her extreme obesity, accepting it as a reflection of her true self. In school, she was enrolled in the usual academic courses—algebra, history, English, and a science. She had not chosen these courses, and she was doing poorly in all of them. Some day, she said, she would like to be a beautician.

Assigning this youngster to academic courses was her school's way of giving her equal opportunity. Equal opportunity for what? It is highly unlikely that she will go to college or even graduate from high school. As of now, she is not being given an equal opportunity for life itself. She needs a course in "popular" science or health—both much denigrated by those who insist on abstract, theoretical, "real" science. She needs to learn that her disease is dangerous, and she needs to learn how to follow an adequate diet, how to exercise, how to do the simple calculations that will allow her to count calories, shop wisely, and interpret her blood pressure and sugar content.

Similarly, if we return to the little boy in Detroit with a toothache, we have to question what sort of equal opportunity he will receive. A compassionate and rational society would see health care, adequate housing, clean air, instruction in parenting, accessible transportation, and genuine physical education as essential parts of equal opportunity. "All children can learn"? Maybe—if they are not sick, suffering toothache, squinting to see the chalkboard, abused at home, breathing air contaminated with lead, worried about a parent in prison, or serving as a caretaker for younger children.

Schools cannot, by themselves, provide equal opportunity. They might come close if they became full-service institutions—providing dental and vision clinics, social services, general health clinics, and child care on campus. But few schools do this, and policymakers just insist that teachers have high expectations for all children—no excuses.

In chapter 2, I mentioned briefly the questionable practice of placing all children in courses called *algebra* or *geometry* that deliver material scarcely recognizable as algebra or geometry. This is a shabby way of claiming to offer equal opportunity. In many urban schools, youngsters are enrolled in such courses, and large numbers of them cannot pass a standardized test in the subjects. Is the answer to strengthen the courses by making them more nearly like traditional courses in academic mathematics? Kids like Joe would still do poorly on the standardized tests. We either have to give up the idea of measuring achievement entirely by tests or provide honestly named courses that will meet the mathematical needs of kids who are not academically inclined. Probably we should do both.

If we follow the first course of action and allow students to receive credit for courses although they fail tests in those courses, we will face the perennial charges of grade inflation and social promotion. We will have to develop powerful and convincing alternative tools of assessment. Given the structure and sequence of academic courses, this may be very difficult. What could convince a college mathematics teacher that a student deserved to pass high school algebra if that student cannot perform the tasks required in college mathematics?

A better alternative is to develop rich courses designed for a wide variety of occupational choices and for everyday life and citizenship. Educators should be held accountable for the quality of these courses, not for getting everyone through the standard academic courses.

Before turning to the topic of accountability, a brief statement of commitment on equality and democracy is in order. A democratic view of equality does not imply equality of aptitudes, achievements, incomes, possessions, or social status. It means, rather, that all competent, adult human beings are recognized as persons capable and worthy of citizenship—that is, participation in the affairs of local, national, and global governance. Occupation, religion, gender, race, wealth, and formal level of education must not constitute or engender any test for this participation. Poor grammar, shabby clothing, dirty fingernails, or halting speech should not diminish the respect owed to a citizen. It is in this Whitmanesque sense that we recognize our interdependence and celebrate our equality. It means also that children should be regarded as apprentice citizens and respected accordingly. Children need practice in the ways of democratic life, and that practice should start early and increase appropriately with age. An education that coerces all children into the same programs and courses is not the best preparation for life in a democratic society.

4

ACCOUNTABILITY

"A CCOUNTABILITY" is another word that appears in our general vocabulary, but its use in education was borrowed directly from the world of business. Readers can check this by surveying several indexes to see when the word first appeared in educational articles. Most of the early citations were from business journals. This heritage does not make *accountability* a tainted word, but it does raise important questions: How does accountability in education differ from accountability in business? Does its use in education neglect concepts that should precede it and give it meaning? Does its use involve certain actual dangers? What are they?

Notice at the outset that we rarely use the word *accountability* in connection with parenting. Parents become accountable to the law when they abuse their children or neglect the basic duties for which parents are thought to be responsible. The motivating concept here is responsibility, and accountability enters the picture only when responsibility has been demonstrably neglected. I will argue that in teaching, as in parenting, responsibility is the fundamental concept on which any reasonable concept of accountability must be built.

Parents are responsible for providing food, shelter, and clothing for their children, but they are not held accountable for the quality or precise standards of food, shelter, or clothing provided. Similarly, among other things, teachers are responsible for their students' learning but, until recently, they have not been held accountable for detailed lists of what is to be learned, nor has it been expected that every student would meet a preset, uniform standard of performance. It has been part of a professional teacher's job to establish variable content and standards for each student and/or group of students. This professional responsibility has sometimes been abused, but it is the abuse that should be abolished, not the broad responsibility.

RESPONSIBILITY

Like parents, but to a lesser degree, teachers are responsible for the overall development of students. They are not directly responsible for food, shelter, clothing, or medical care, but today they are responsible for observing and reporting neglect in these basic areas. In their daily work, many of us would argue, they are directly responsible for development of the "whole child" or "whole person"; that is, teachers are rightly expected to promote not only intellectual development but also social, emotional, physical, ethical, and aesthetic development. In addition, some of us (even some agnostics and atheists) believe that teachers should support spiritual development in the form of intelligent belief or unbelief.

Most good teachers feel these responsibilities keenly. However, they do not expect to be held accountable for, say, emotional development unless they are guilty of some form of cruelty. Teachers who regularly use sarcasm, threats, or humiliation are rightly called on to explain their behavior and to cease using such tactics. But no one, as yet, has suggested that teachers should be rated on some scale that measures the emotional well-being or growth of their students. They are held accountable only in the event of alleged negligence of a widely accepted general responsibility.

Responsibility is a much deeper, wider ranging concept than accountability. Typically, a worker or teacher is accountable to some higher authority, and accountability can often be satisfied by conformity, compliance with the letter of the law. In contrast, responsibility points downward in the hierarchy. As teachers, we are responsible for those below us—those for whom we serve as authorities. Teachers may be *accountable* to administrators for certain outcomes, but they are *responsible* to their students for a host of outcomes. Many of these outcomes are not easily measured.

Teachers understand that certain long-standing norms—some of them tacit—are in place, and that they have a responsibility to uphold them. Consider, for example, norms of classroom control. Generally, we expect classrooms to be quiet places in which work is pursued conscientiously, but teachers are not often held to an explicit standard of classroom noise or quiet. The norm becomes active when a classroom gets noisy. Then the teacher may be asked to account for the noise. A good supervisor will be satisfied (even pleased) to learn that the students are preparing scenery and props for a school play—hence the noise of construction, conversation, and laughter. A supervisor who holds a narrow view of education may simply demand quiet and put an end to the creative activity. In such situations, teachers become accountable for maintaining an explicit standard of quiet. In more genuinely educational situations, they are simply asked to explain the deviation from a widely accepted norm. Among the most thoughtful educators, the norm itself may be questioned.

A few years ago, as a consulting member of a consortium on character education, I attended a meeting at which principals from participating schools reported on their programs. A middle school principal reported proudly that his school had finally achieved "silent halls." Children were forbidden to talk as they changed classes, and the rule seemed to be working. He and his faculty were now going to press for quiet lunchrooms.

I was flabbergasted. Why in the world would anyone want silent halls? When were these youngsters allowed to talk with one another? And teachers were expected to stand outside their classrooms and remind students as they passed, "No talking!" Teachers in this school were accountable for maintaining a standard of silence. This is one example—unfortunately, I've since encountered many more—of accountability gone wrong, entirely at odds with basic teaching responsibilities.

Teachers, like parents, are expected to take their responsibilities seriously, but they have not usually been held accountable for specific, detailed outcomes. Teachers have been expected to use professional judgment in selecting and promoting such outcomes. If outcomes fall far short of reasonable expectations, teachers are rightly called to account for the shortfall.

I got my first job teaching high school mathematics at midyear because the teacher I replaced was totally ineffective at getting the kids to learn algebra. A standardized test had been given at midyear, and the results had been deplorable. The teacher was fired, I was hired, and the kids started to learn algebra. Most of them did learn algebra, and scores at the end of the year were respectable.

Teachers obviously have a major responsibility for student learning, and most teachers take this responsibility seriously. If, through incompetence or negligence, student learning is demonstrably deficient, teachers should expect to be held accountable. But when we ask people to account for the results of their work, we should listen to the explanations they offer. There may be something in the system, the particular school, or the community that stands in the way of student learning. For what, beyond the satisfaction of normal expectations, should teachers be held accountable? And what are "normal" expectations?

ACCOUNTABILITY AND LEARNING

In the business world, accountability always centers on profit. Other factors are involved—appropriate use of money, quality of product, satisfaction of customers, efficiency of production, stability of labor force—but all of these others are focused ultimately on profit. It was predictable, then, that accountability in education would focus on some form of bottom line. That line has now been defined as student achievement measured by standardized tests. One could protest here that establishing student achievement as the bottom line need not have implied that achievement be measured by standardized tests. That seems right, and many educators are arguing for broader, stronger measures.

But even deciding straightaway on achievement as the schools' bottom line is too swift a move. In past decades (indeed, past centuries), educators, philosophers, and other parties interested in education have discussed aims, purposes, and responsibilities. Talk about aims has largely disappeared from today's discussion of schooling. It is as though we have decided that there is one aim of education: to produce high achievement scores. We should question this decision.

With test scores established as the bottom line, educators are pressed to concentrate on those subjects—those *parts* of subjects—that will be tested. Contradictions and anomalies pop up everywhere. For example, schools still claim some responsibility for educating citizens for life in a democratic society, and most people identify this task with social studies; yet social studies is regularly sacrificed to instruction in reading and mathematics. Accountability, unreflectively defined, can arbitrarily and dangerously narrow the curriculum.

Attention to aims would encourage us to ask just what schools might do to produce democratic citizens. There would be debate over the importance of civic knowledge, history, social studies more broadly construed, and hands-on experience in democratic life. Some of us would point out that a great strength of the comprehensive high school has been its provision of extracurricular activities that bring together students with different interests and academic aptitudes. In these activities, students elect leaders, set goals, make plans for implementation, act on their plans, and evaluate their success. They engage in a form of democratic life. Reflection on the centrality of band, student government, art, drama, clubs, sports, and other such activities that provide practice in democratic living might well culminate in a commitment to continue support for them. We would have identified their usefulness in promoting an important aim—citizenship.

I am not going to argue that test scores have no place in a scheme of accountability. They do. But what exactly is that place? The mathematics teacher I replaced failed in her responsibility as a teacher, and that failure was confirmed by test scores. She could not maintain order in the classroom, and her students were not learning. Rightly, she was held accountable for this failure.

Mathematics teachers are responsible for teaching and getting most students to learn some mathematics. But there is more to student learning than achieving respectable test scores. A good math teacher knows that only part of learning is captured in test scores. What is revealed in projects and reports? Are the kids learning anything about the place of mathematics in history? Do they know that they live in a mathematicized world? Do any of the kids have a sense of mathematical elegance? Are they invited to do problems and proofs in several ways? Have they learned to overcome test and math anxiety? Are they developing genuine intellectual curiosity? Can they communicate their ideas? Do they treat one another with respect? Are they looking forward to another course in mathematics?

Let's pause for a moment and review the questions just asked. Should all students learn something about the place of mathematics in history? Should some learn more than others? Surely, some students will be more interested in historical studies than others, and they should have opportunities to engage in such studies. Do all (or most) understand that they live in a mathematicized world? Can they describe what that means? Probably every student should know that insurance rates and other financial indicators vary by locality. Must all students appreciate mathematical elegance? This would seem a silly demand when so many students fail to understand the basic idea of mathematical proof. But a good math teacher would feel irresponsible if she did not expose her most talented students to the idea and invite them to watch for examples of mathematical beauty and elegance. As we consider math anxiety, we note that not all students suffer from it, but we feel a special responsibility to relieve it in those who do. How about intellectual curiosity? If we are serious about the development of intellectual curiosity, we will have to reach into realms other than mathematics, and good math teachers accept a responsibility to do this. Scores on a standardized math test will not tell us what a teacher has done to encourage intellectual curiosity in the arts, literature, science, history, or a host of subjects that can be related to mathematics. Similarly, test scores will not tell us how students have grown (or deteriorated) as citizens or as considerate peers under this teacher's tutelage.

The math department at the school where I taught used standardized tests at the end of every school year. We used them to check on how we were doing, and every year we met as a department to discuss possible reasons why the scores were better or worse, but the scores were not held against the kids. The only high stakes involved were for teachers like the one I replaced—people who were demonstrably incompetent.

Today there are high stakes attached to tests for kids, teachers, administrators, and schools. We regularly hear about fourth graders who suffer sleeplessness, nausea, and anxiety before these tests. Some children even vomit on the tests. The pressure is especially keen in districts where children know that they might be retained in grade if they fail the tests. Schools, insofar as they are institutions of education, should be held accountable for these results, too. School practices that literally make children sick should be discontinued.

We should want our children to develop as whole people—intellectually, morally, socially, emotionally, artistically, spiritually. They should not be treated as commodities for the labor and consumer markets. But unfortunately the overemphasis on grades and test scores may do exactly that. Indeed, the usual way of reporting scores does this dramatically well: *Fourth graders did better this year in math.* Better? In what way "better"? Who did better? How did last year's fourth graders do in 5th grade? In particular, how much better (or worse) did Patti do? Where does the individual, whole child appear in such reporting?

There is another crucially important issue to be addressed when we talk about increasing achievement or learning. Many psychologists make a distinction between learning in the narrow sense of responding to a stimulus with the required answer and developmental learning. The former usually occurs when learning is aimed at a specific goal, such as passing a test. I've called this the "telephone number" problem. When we wish to make a call, we look up the relevant number and, if nothing interrupts us, we remember it long enough to punch in the digits. Afterward, unless this is a number we will use frequently, we rightly and promptly forget it. When our purpose has been served, there is no point in remembering much information. It is probably this phenomenon that accounts for the fact that many adults can recall so little information about American history. Critics accuse the schools of failing to teach the material, but schools do teach it. Students simply find no reason to remember it.

Like so many topics we must address here, this one is complex. Narrow learning, massed practice, and intensive drill are not always useless. In mathematics, they can facilitate important learning by helping to routinize frequently used skills. When a skill or bit of information (such as the ABCs) will be used again and again, narrow learning is efficient, but when we seek to change habits of mind, induce critical thinking, or encourage deep understanding, it won't do. As teachers, we are responsible for, and should be accountable for (i.e., asked to explain and justify), our means as well as our ends. The test-driven approach so common today may actually undermine lasting, developmental learning.

Closely connected to the reliance on narrow learning is the practice of using behavioral objectives—learning objectives that state exactly what students will learn, under what conditions, and to what degree of proficiency. (I'll say more about behavioral objectives and their history in the chapter on standards.) Stating exactly what students are expected to do as a result of instruction can be pedagogically economical, and entirely justified if we are aiming at skills to be routinized. But when we structure whole units of study and sometimes whole curricula this way, we deprive students of the lasting learning that should result from creating their own purposes and structures of subject matter. When I was a high school student, if one of my classmates asked, "What will be on the test?" the answer often was, "Everything." Granted, this answer proved discouraging to many students. But for others of us, it forced a gradual and continuous intellectual development. We had to review, interpret, assess what was important, organize, and create our own outlines and summaries. And it is these tasks that lead to lasting learning— to intellectual habits of mind. Incidentally, as part of the process, many of the facts that could have been deliberately and briefly committed to memory were fitted thoughtfully into a long-lasting structure and were thus remembered long after school tests were behind us. Telling students, through narrowly stated behavioral objectives, exactly what they must learn and do removes the necessity to develop intellectual habits of mind. The practice reduces intellectual life to mental labor.

We should not depend too heavily on test scores. Educators should ask, What has Johnny learned? and not simply, Has Johnny learned X? We can specify certain concepts, definitions, and skills to be learned, but these represent only the building blocks of lasting learning, and they will themselves be forgotten rapidly if not used regularly. To find out what students are learning, there must be time for free reading, discussion, projects of short and long duration, opportunities to grapple with problems that may not yield solutions. There must be choice built into the curriculum. Dewey argued that students should be involved in the formation of purposes for their own learning. From an array of acceptable possibilities, they should have opportunities to choose which they will pursue. These choices are in themselves important information for caring teachers. In addition to common learnings, each student should learn some things that others may not learn. What has Johnny learned? is a powerful question, and it cannot be entirely answered by the results of standardized testing.

At present, many high-stakes tests are a mishmash of essential and trivial elements. Many reasonably successful adults would be unable to answer some of the questions on 8th-grade tests. Why, then, should high stakes be attached to such tests? We have not taken the time to study carefully what information and skills are necessary for everyone. We have even neglected some principles of test construction. It was once assumed that responsible test-makers would arrange test items in order of difficulty. Now, with billions of dollars pouring into test construction, many tests are deficient in basic test psychology. It is not unusual for the very first questions to be difficult and to require skills and information not basic to what is being tested. The first questions on one state's 8th-grade mathematics test, for example, require a fairly high level of reading ability. Indeed, on this test, there is no question—not one—that does not require reading skills. How can we know from such a test whether or not a child has learned to use basic arithmetic algorithms? Teachers in the state using that test told me that more than a few students get zero on the test. As a diagnostic tool, the test is useless. For an old math teacher (like me), the questions appear at first quite interesting. They will challenge students who know some math and read well. But the results tell us nothing about students' weaknesses and nothing about their possible strengths. Kids who have worked hard to learn the basic processes get no chance to show that they have mastered these processes. As educators we should hold ourselves accountable for accepting such tests as measures of our students' achievement. Our acceptance of bad tests represents a dereliction of duty—of responsibility to our students.

In holding teachers and schools accountable for student learning, policymakers should have reasonable expectations, and they should be asked to give evidence that their expectations are indeed reasonable. Teachers and parents should not be bullied into accepting false expectations. Slogans such as "the soft bigotry of low expectations" cause us to soft-pedal our objections, and then we are hit by "No excuses!" But there are sound reasons why teachers should not be expected to bring all students up to a preset standard in specific subjects. *Universal proficiency* may be, as some critics have charged, an oxymoron.

The high school at which I replaced a teacher at midyear was an average small town school. On most tests given at the time (including SATs), our students' average scores were at about the national average. We had some excellent students, some poor ones, many average ones. There was a legitimate reason to expect that most of the students enrolled in algebra would achieve at or near the average. That expectation was not met by the teacher who was replaced. It is also important to note that the students in my classes elected to take algebra; they were not required to do so.

Suppose now that a teacher is faced with a very different situation. Students in her school (with a few exceptions) have never done well in algebra. In the past, relatively few elected to take algebra. Now they are all required to take it. If an algebra pretest were administered (as it should be), most students would do very poorly. Is the teacher to be held accountable if her students fail a state-administered test at the end of the school year? Is it true that "all children can learn" algebra, and that if they fail to do so, it is the teacher's or school's fault?

This conclusion is preposterous, and yet it is one that NCLB suggests. Urban schools all over the United States are grappling with this problem. Afraid to say that another form of mathematics might be more useful for many children, they insist—in the name of equality—that all children will now be "offered" algebra. As I mentioned earlier, the result is a spate of pseudo-algebra courses, which (if passed) will make students' transcripts acceptable for college admission but will in no way prepare students adequately for college mathematics.

What are teachers to do? Most teachers, deeply concerned about their students, choose topics that their students can handle but, in doing so, they know that they are not teaching "real" algebra. They are understandably torn between insisting on a rigorous course that most of their students would fail and compromising in order to keep students in school and help them to graduate. They are harshly criticized by people who say that we do students no favor when we let them graduate from high school without the knowledge and skills "they will need." But, in fact, we *do* do students a favor when we help them to graduate from high school. The credential itself, not what graduates actually know, makes a difference both in lifetime earnings and in the likelihood that they will seek further education. Further, we have not given nearly enough thought to what students "will need" after high school. There is little reason to suppose that the same preparation will suffice for both work (and its many varieties) and college (and its many varieties).

If I were teaching high school mathematics today, I would do as many of my beleaguered colleagues are doing. I would come as close to real algebra as I could without causing enormous failure and discouragement. I would talk honestly with my students about the problems we share, including the confession that what they are learning from me will not be enough to smooth the road to college. My daily message would, nevertheless, be, "Don't give up. Hang in there. We'll get through this."

It would be better, of course, if students could choose alternative math courses that would prepare them for work or a postsecondary course of training. Perversely, mouthing equality, we show contempt for the many students who might proudly enter well-paying but nonacademic forms of work and study, and we thereby deprive them of real opportunities. The actual message, rarely voiced frankly, is "Go to college or be nothing." Our students and our democratic way of life both suffer as a result.

Good teachers recognize that their responsibilities differ with different groups of students. When math teachers greet a class of students who have elected to take our course because they love the subject, we know there will not be a problem with standardized tests. Our responsibilities broaden and deepen. We can explore history, biography, literature, architecture, music, art, economics, philosophy, psychology, religion—whatever interests various subgroups and individuals. We can skip most of the simple exercises and go straight to the more challenging ones. We are working with intrinsic motivation, and we have a great responsibility to increase our own competence—and our students'—in the subject and in general scholarship.

If students are not greatly interested in our subject but plan to go to college, we have another form of motivation with which to work. Chances are that they will work hard so long as failure or the fear of failure does not grip them. Our job is to build skills patiently, insist on mastery of the basics to avoid future difficulties, and show an interest in the subjects and topics that really interest our students. With good humor, we let students know that many nice, successful people have hated math, that we hope they will hate it less as a result of their experience with us, and that we will help. But we do not feel responsible for providing the options we offer to students with an intrinsic interest in math. Indeed, it would be insensitive to insist that all students are really interested in math, need only to be inspired, and so on. The self-worth of our students should not depend on their embracing our interests.

Finally, there are the students who have no interest in either math or college. Some have talked about going to college in much the way that third graders talk about becoming doctors or fire fighters. They have no real idea what it takes to be well prepared for college, and they resent being forced into subjects they hate and find irrelevant. With such youngsters, we should provide intensive counseling and genuine choice. There should be fine vocational courses that lead to further training in postsecondary institutions, and perhaps there should be 6-year high school academic programs for students who want to prepare for college but are woefully unprepared when they enter high school. Simply insisting that teachers will bring all students to proficiency in every required subject is analogous to demanding that physicians eliminate death in everyone under age 80. It is ridiculous and will lead to the demise of genuine education.

ACCOUNTABILITY AND HEALTH AND SAFETY

Schools are responsible for the health and safety of students within their walls. On health, accountability measures are necessarily conditional. It would be preposterous to hold schools accountable for bringing all students to predetermined standards of health, such as freedom from disease or disability or attainment of standard weight or height. And again, accountability is applied mainly in the breach. The presence of broken railings, torn carpets, lead paint, or asbestos can lead to accidents or illness, and schools must remove all known causes of such problems.

But as we saw earlier, schools do not often connect their curricula to the general, everyday problems of health. The Bronx teenager suffering from diabetes was required to study algebra and history; she learned nothing in school about her disease, its causes, or its treatment. Many schools do offer a one-semester (rarely a full year) course in health, and many more require a course called Physical Education/Health, but typically little time is spent on topics of general health, and even courses in physical education have been reduced to a minimum in many schools. Students may be required to participate in a brief course on sex education, driver education, or drug education but, when they have "had" the course, they go on to other things. There is no continuous concentration on health as there is on English and mathematics.

Looking at this situation, we are moved to return to the basic question: For what should schools be held accountable? Or better: For what should schools take some responsibility? And what form should that responsibility take? I cannot explore these profound questions here, but I want to point out that educators and policymakers should be exploring them, and at present, too few are engaged in this exploration.

NCLB requires schools to report on issues of safety. Concern for the safety of students and teachers is certainly defensible. But as we consider measures designed to increase safety, we should also consider what may be lost by adopting certain recommendations. Again, we must reject the single-mindedness that currently afflicts our approach to educational aims. We want our students to be safe, yes. But what if the safety measures we adopt actually get in the way of other legitimate goals?

Consider the recommendations made by a visiting committee to one high school in Virginia. Prominent among them were the following:

- The computerized disciplinary file system should be on a network so that the principal and assistant principals have immediate access to the data.
- Trees at the entrance of the student parking lot should be removed to provide clear visibility.
- All adults within the school should constantly check exterior doors to make sure they are locked.
- Administrators, faculty, staff, and students should be issued picture identification cards at the beginning of the school year. (Thayer, 1996, p. 288).

It may be useful to have a computerized disciplinary file system; it would surely help, given an incident, in "rounding up the usual suspects." But it would be even better if the principals and assistant principals got to know the kids as individuals. Many discipline problems can be prevented by caring human contact.

Next, it is sad to recommend the removal of trees. Do we want our kids to live in Foucault's panopticon—under continuous surveillance from some central point? Parents, teachers, and students should, perhaps, spend time together planting trees, not chopping them down. There should be class meetings, discussions, and exploration of alternatives. What responsibility do we each have for keeping our campus both safe and beautiful?

And why must all exterior doors be locked? Are there really bad people who might come in and commit crimes or disrupt legitimate activities? (Sometimes there are, and then the locking of doors is necessary.) Are we afraid parents will sneak in? More likely, the fear is that kids will sneak out. To prevent this, we make sure that, if they do, they can't get back in.

Picture ID's? Well, we live in an age where such measures are necessary, but we shouldn't suppose that they will solve major problems of human interaction. We need to arrange our schools so that people have opportunities to recognize one another and so that relations of care and trust can be developed. Smaller schools might help to do this.

We cannot turn the clock back to earlier days, and earlier days were far from perfect. However, when my husband and I were in high school there were no locked doors, no security guards, no tags (or metal detectors) on library books, no ID cards; we had a full hour for lunch and eight additional periods of classes. I am not suggesting that we simply (and irresponsibly) remove current safeguards. I am suggesting that we analyze, reflect, study, and come together for regular discussion on these matters. Why have conditions changed so drastically? We are, after all, at least partly responsible for current conditions. What can we do to make them more humane?

In this chapter, I have called for a comprehensive and continuous examination of educational responsibilities and an approach to accountability based on such an examination. The topic remains incomplete, however, without a discussion of the specific subject matter for which schools today are held accountable. We turn next to the topic of standards.

5

STANDARDS

T HE WORD *standard* is used today in a variety of ways. In education, its use as a mere label for content is perhaps most baffling. In what way, for example, should "Number and Operations" be regarded as a standard? Today's educational literature is filled with lists of such topics, announced as standards. Why are we calling statements of content *standards*? What is to be gained by this move?

I'll organize this chapter around the labels used by Diane Ravitch: content standards, performance standards, and opportunity- to- learn standards. I'll give more space to the first, content standards, not because they are most important but because there is so much to uncover in their analysis. In closing, I'll emphasize the need for variable standards—an idea that goes against the whole current movement.

CONTENT STANDARDS

Readers who look carefully at current standards will spot an important problem almost immediately. Instead of naming a topic or area of subject matter, standards specify exactly what teachers are expected to teach, and there is little acknowledgement of differences in students' abilities or interests. Indeed, many documents on standards insist that there is no conflict between equity and excellence and insist on "mathematics for all" or "science for all." But clearly, if we establish uniform standards in a given subject—topics, skills, concepts, processes—we will deprive our best students of opportunities to achieve excellence surpassing those standards, and we will also deprive students with other talents from achieving excellence in their own areas of interest.

I cannot undertake here an analysis of curriculum recommendations in historical context, but interested readers should take the time to read the recommendations that emerged in the 1950s and 1960s and compare them with current recommendations. The former frankly differentiated between college preparatory and non–college preparatory work and between average students and those with exceptional talent. Excellence was, properly, defined in context.

Such contextual definition does not necessitate shoddy courses for the less academically talented (although, as I have admitted, that often happened). It implies, rather, that teachers must use judgment to decide among a variety of legitimate options for individuals and for groups of students. For example, in the 2nd-year algebra and trigonometry course that I taught, our text provided A, B, and C exercises, with A representing the most basic material and C the most challenging. Some of my students were required to do only the A exercises, and some were excused entirely from these and went directly to a few Bs and all of the Cs. This course was a 3rd-year course in college preparatory mathematics, and yet the differences in interest and aptitude were enormous. In a general mathematics course that I also taught, there were students who could not add two fractions and a few who had not yet learned how to use an ordinary ruler. Imagine how ridiculous it would have been to establish the same standards for all of these students.

Supporters of an identical, high-quality curriculum for all students will challenge me here. They will argue that the situation I have described is exactly what they want to change. No child should get to high school without learning how to add two fractions or use a ruler. I applaud the sentiment, and I agree that we should do a better job in elementary schools. But no matter what we do, some children will find traditional academic work unpalatable, and many will have difficulty meeting the artificial timelines set for 3rd grade or 7th grade. We cannot help children by simply demanding that they meet grade-level standards, nor are they helped by retaining them in grade. My most important point, however, is one that I will emphasize repeatedly: Excellence is defined in context. An academic curriculum replete with physics, chemistry, and higher math may or may not be excellent. A commercial curriculum that prepares students directly for business may or may nor be excellent. A vocational curriculum may or may not be excellent. The notion that an excellent curriculum for all must be an academic curriculum that prepares students for traditional college work is not a democratic notion, and it degrades the very idea of excellence. It undermines respect for a multitude of human talents and displays a frightening lack of appreciation for the rich diversity of occupational life. It works against an understanding of contemporary interdependence.

Because this is such a controversial topic, I want to say a little more about my agreement with those who want to improve learning so that kids do not enter high school unable to add fractions, read ordinary written material, or use acceptable English in speaking. I think we can accomplish these goals if we work on them sensibly. But we won't do it by insisting, in the name of equality, on establishing a host of questionable standards for all students. We have to study, analyze, and discuss the skills that are essential for success in further schooling, and make sure that kids acquire these skills. This means working with individual students—encouraging, supporting, and assisting them. It does not mean imposing the same test on everyone, punishing those who fail by holding them back (thereby ensuring further failure), and penalizing schools for failing to reach impossible goals. It also means allowing sufficient time to instruct, encourage, and guide students who find these tasks difficult. Rushing on, reluctant to deprive students of a host of trivial "standards," we risk failing to attain those goals that are really important. Obviously, it also means culling the junk that presently clutters the school curriculum and is given dignity by its appearance on standardized tests.

It remains possible that content standards as they are now written might include the potential for differentiation. When "patterns, functions, and algebra" is listed as a standard, both content and performance remain largely open. We can agree that all students should learn something in this large area of mathematical study. But why do we call such a topic a standard?

As I write this, I have before me earlier essays on goals for school mathematics. The topics listed in a 1959 publication of the Commission on Mathematics differ very little from those found in a recent statement of the National Council of Teachers of Mathematics (NCTM), but they are frankly aimed at college preparation. There are two major differences between the two documents: First, the NCTM document has much more detail, and it is in that detail that curriculum options are lost. Second, the NCTM document refuses to differentiate between college preparation and preparation for work. Indeed, it brushes aside the possibility of providing rich work-preparatory courses, calling such programs a series of dead-end tracks. The writers are correct that such courses have too often been exactly that—dead ends. But they could be excellent courses. And the pseudo-algebra courses we are now inflicting on students are just as bad.

Use of the word *standard* for topic, concept, or skill is meant to convey a twin sense of uniformity and high quality, but the resulting masses of standards are really elaborate tables of contents and far too specific to be used with all students. The underlying intent is to standardize, that is, to move in the direction of one comprehensive table of contents for each approved ("standard") course and one set of standardized courses. At present, such standards are set at the state level, but there is a strong push to nationalize content standards.

Today's way of talking about content has a history. In the early 1960s, the use of behavioral objectives became popular. Sometimes these objectives were referred to as *instructional objectives*, but the idea was to convert all objectives for instruction into the preferred behavioral form. Lesson plans were no longer supposed to emphasize what the teacher would do but, rather, what students were expected to do as a result of instruction. A properly written behavioral objective was one that stated exactly what students would do, to what level of proficiency, and under what sort of assessment. For example:

> Students will add fractions with denominators up to 12,
> with accuracy of at least 80%
> on a paper and pencil test of 10 exercises.

There is certainly clarity in such statements, and sometimes that clarity is helpful; in other cases, it begs the question.

Some years ago, I worked briefly with a large group of 5th-grade teachers in Arizona. They raised questions about an instructional objective the district insisted on using; the objective was almost identical to the one above. One teacher said, "Look, Nel, we've always known that we're supposed to get kids to add such fractions. The question is how to do it." For these teachers, in this situation, clarity was not the issue. The clarity was, in fact, misleading, making a difficult task seem easy.

However, as I said earlier, almost all teachers find behavioral objectives useful for some purposes. At least tacitly (the precise statement may or may not be useful), when we teach a specific skill, we go straight at it, and we test our students without adding any complications. We want to know whether our instruction on this particular procedure has been effective. As a math teacher, I always expected that nearly all of my students would achieve 80% or better on a quiz testing a specific, limited skill. If they did not, I discarded the quiz and retaught the material. On comprehensive tests requiring problem identification and solution, my classes never achieved such results, and I did not expect them to do so. The real pedagogical challenge is to figure out when to use behavioral objectives and when to use another approach.

I want to spend some time on this very important question, but first let's finish up the brief recent historical look at the transition from behavioral objectives to standards. It became clear to educators that there were problems with the attempt to write curriculum entirely in terms of behavioral objectives, and most school districts abandoned the attempt. But the behavioral objectives movement was a precursor to what we call today content and performance standards.

The approach was modified some when the language of behavioral objectives gave way to *competencies*. The idea was the same; instruction was to be guided by a clear statement of what students should be able to do as a result of that instruction. The language was somewhat eased and made more natural. Teachers were now allowed to use "understand" and "be able to"—both forbidden under strict behavioral objectives because they do not specify the observable behaviors that would allow us to claim that an objective has been met.

Content standards are in the same mode. The change in language is at least partly motivated by a desire to fit the approach into the contemporary language of standards. The language also paves the road to standardization. It is thus not a trivial change. Labeling "numbers and operations" and "patterns, functions, and algebra" as standards instead of topics or subjects signals complicity with a movement that insists on filling those standards out with particular outcomes. It is reasonable and helpful to have a list—a table of contents—for any course to be taught. But curriculum supervisors and teachers must be free to use professional judgment on the subtopics and skills that will be taught to various groups and individuals. To fill out these standards with detailed sublists for *all* students is a highly questionable move. To suppose that every class period can be directed by an objective thus detailed is to invite a serious corruption of teaching. Among the dangers are the following:

1. Narrowing learning
2. Failing to introduce potentially interesting topics (exposure)
3. Failing to identify individual students' varying personal motivations
4. Missing chances to connect with other subjects
5. Missing chances for collateral learning
6. Making life dull for teachers

Let us consider these dangers—and remedies—in greater detail.

A great danger is the one discussed in Chapter 4—that all learning will be reduced to the narrow learning designed to induce correct responses on tests. To call such learning *narrow* is not to demean it. Learning to factor trinomials is a prerequisite for adding algebraic fractions. If adding algebraic fractions is important (and this is a big if), then learning to factor trinomials is an essential bit of narrow learning. But notice that this is not a skill that affects life outside algebra class. Unless one enters an occupation that requires the regular use of algebraic fractions, nothing follows from learning these skills. Most such skills are quickly forgotten.

In contrast, spending some time on insurance rates and doing some associated calculations can help students to understand that where they live may affect their car insurance and that legal representatives may put a price on a teenager's life, using his or her high school grades as a prediction of lifetime earnings. Something real, something connected to life (as Alfred North Whitehead recommended) follows from this study. All students should come to some understanding of what it means to live in a mathematicized world, and this understanding is not best encouraged through behavioral objectives, although a teacher may use such objectives to give students practice in figuring percentages, reading tables, and the like. Notice also that the selection of topics should depend on the interests of the students.

We may fail to introduce potentially interesting topics. A powerful argument can be made for exposure to knowledge as an aim of education, the outcome of which may be awareness rather than learning in the strict sense. We have heard of some things, although we know little more about them. Exposure to an idea, story, or name will lead some students to pursue further knowledge with enthusiasm. Other students will just let it slide by. Years later, a former student may respond to someone's remark, "I remember Ms. Smith mentioning that," and the reminder may lead to renewed curiosity. Exposure to a host of ideas encourages a great variation in interests and achievement in high school students who have been well taught. One might argue that the great benefit of formal schooling is precisely that it exposes students to worthwhile ideas that they might otherwise miss entirely. If we want only to teach the skills that students, in their youthful naivety, seek, we could go ahead and "deschool" society. Employing specific instructional objectives every day for every lesson may sacrifice the benefits of exposure. Recognizing the potential benefits of exposure, a teacher might develop a lesson around ideas that he or she would like to share with students. Some of the students will pick up on one idea, others on a different one. There is no one response or skill expected of everyone as a result of such a lesson. It is an invitation—a free gift from a knowledgeable teacher to curious students. Should we give up such lessons? This discussion is another reminder that we must consider inputs as well as outcomes. Much of what a teacher "puts in" or offers will result in differential outcomes.

We may distort the notion of motivation. When we say that "students will do X" as a result of our instruction, we often forget to add, "if they want to." Every teacher is at the mercy of student motivation. It is sometimes insisted that teachers must motivate their students. However, it would seem more compatible with preparation for life in a liberal democracy, to identify students' existing motivations and try to connect one's teaching to those. Attending to student motives and teaching for exposure (or awareness) are related. Teachers need to consider a range of student motives. There actually are people motivated by the love of mathematics? Wow! Exposure to the possibility of such a motive does not imply that a teacher must produce this motive in her students as an outcome of instruction. A student may legitimately react by saying, "That's the way I feel about baseball." Notice, too, that teaching for exposure and listening to students' reactions helps us to understand their motives and interests.

Some lessons, then, are guided by the desire to identify existing motives or to inspire new ones. But we do not insist that a particular motive be displayed in student behavior. There is nothing to test as a result of such lessons. There is, however, much to analyze and evaluate in reflection.

We may miss opportunities to connect with other subjects. One day in a general math class, the students and I were discussing a problem involving the cost of gasoline for a cross-country trip. Typically, all the required figures were given, but I wanted to make the problem a bit more real, and I suggested, "Let's think about how we'd plan this trip. We're here in New Jersey and we're headed to California. What states will we go through?" No answer. "Well, what's the first one we'll pass through?" Amazingly, the answers included everything from Georgia to Nebraska, plus a few cities. I wanted to pull down a map and take a vicarious trip across the country. But this was a math classroom, and there was no map.

School planning should include provision of resources that help to connect subject matters. There should be U.S. and world maps, computers, and dictionaries in every classroom, and teachers should be encouraged to depart from their immediate subject into other subjects. Teachers should be models of educated persons, not simply machines to "deliver instruction."

We may miss chances for incidental, or collateral, learning. This danger is different from the risk of abandoning the aim of exposing students to a variety of ideas, not just the ones they will be tested on. Incidental learning occurs in the course of conversation, as ideas are being developed. Incidental learning takes place without its being specified as an aim or objective. It is the kind of learning that occurs daily in good homes. Children from such homes pick up all sorts of things that are not purposely taught. Much incidental learning happens in free reading. We learn many things that surprise and delight us when we read for pleasure, although it is not usually our intention to learn these particular items. Obviously, we cannot depend on incidental learning for an entire curriculum, but it is shortsighted to eliminate the possibility of incidental learning by specifying one narrow objective for each lesson. It is good now and then (quite often, actually) to get off the main road and travel the byways, letting knowledge stick to us like burrs in the field, as Robert Frost described the poet's way of acquiring knowledge.

We risk making teaching dull for teachers. Many of us could not imagine teaching day in and day out to a specific, narrowly defined objective. Preparation for teaching at its best is a deeply engaging intellectual activity. Good teachers review old material, learn new material, and bring refreshing new ideas to their lessons. They prepare themselves, not simply their lessons. Ideas, anecdotes, applications, and connections pile up during such preparation. It wouldn't be possible to include all of this material in any one lesson, but it is stored up in teachers for use if the occasion arises. For me, the continuing opportunity to learn provided by the task of preparation is one of the great joys of teaching. The kind of learning produced by specific objectives properly serves larger purposes, and teachers must be prepared to extend and share these purposes.

Excellence is properly evaluated in context. It must be possible for teachers to adjust objectives—to add, delete, or revise them. In the era of behavioral objectives, teachers were told never to drop an objective but to change their teaching methods to reach the objective with every student. Today we are making the same foolish demand, with an added command: No excuses! I argue that to the contrary, good teachers should be ready to discard or replace some objectives for some or all students, and they should accept responsibility for doing so.

PERFORMANCE STANDARDS

Everyone who has gone to school is familiar with the idea of performance standards. To get an A, students have to achieve a certain score or accumulate a certain number of points. Each letter grade is defined in specific terms, usually in numbers.

At the national level, reading, math, and science tests sponsored by the National Assessment of Educational Progress (NAEP) are given to a large sample of students in grades 4, 8, and 12. Results of the tests are scored "below basic," "basic," "proficient," or "advanced." In addition to the national test, states have their own tests (as is mandated by NCLB), and these are graded in a similar way—that is, the evaluative labels are the same. For purposes of reporting under NCLB, the emphasis in each state is on the percentage of students rated "proficient." Many studies have shown that there is often a large gap between the number of students judged proficient on the NAEP tests and the number judged proficient on the state tests. Both the state tests themselves and the marks required for the designation "proficient" vary widely, sometimes by as much as 50%. Almost certainly, the NAEP tests are too hard, but many of the state tests are too easy.

A few years ago, one state superintendent of schools commented publicly that his state's tests had to be upgraded. They were too easy, he said: "Too many kids are passing them." That remark was made just seven or eight years ago. Many people agreed that the tests should be harder. We should have higher standards. But, at the same time, teachers are expected to teach so well that all students pass the harder tests. Again, there is little serious discussion of what all students should know and what subgroups of students (depending on their interests and aptitudes) should know. Why should the tests be made harder? What might be gained by this move? What might be lost? Simply suggesting that tests be made harder is just foolish. Consider the contradictions that arise: Make the tests harder but get all students to pass them; if all students pass them, raise a cry about grade inflation; then make the tests harder, and so on.

Good teachers—teachers well trained in test construction as well as pedagogy—know that the greater part of any test should address the basic material to be tested. For example, a unit test in algebra might consist of ten questions, the first seven of which would require knowledge of material basic to mastery of the unit. The last three would be increasingly challenging, and fewer students would answer them satisfactorily. In the best instructional situations, students who could not pass such a test would receive additional instruction, and then take the test again. Those who not only passed but excelled would go on to the next unit and also be encouraged to pursue individual topics or projects.

When I worked with a team teaching 2nd-year algebra through a continuous progress approach, we ended the year with a dramatic spread in achievement. Some students passed a minimal course consisting of six units; these students succeeded (with difficulty) in passing just one unit test each marking period. Most students passed a standard course of nine or ten units, qualifying them for a rigorous 4th year of college preparatory mathematics. And an impressive number passed sixteen units—the entire fat textbook plus some work in more advanced mathematics. All students received credit for the course, and on a standardized test at the end of the year, none of our students scored in the lowest decile nationally.

It might seem, from the account just given, that I recommend holding back students until they can pass certain grade-level tests. But in fact I am adamantly opposed to retention in grade. Holding students back should be used only in short-term situations and only for the purpose of ensuring the possibility of some success in the next unit of study. Repeating a whole year's work is worthless; it is demoralizing and ineffective. Often students who are held back do even worse the second time.

This method for teaching 2nd-year algebra is an adaptation of Benjamin Bloom's (1968) mastery learning. It incorporates the idea that short-term evaluation, diagnosis, and tailored instruction can be used to bring most students to a level of performance that will, at the least, permit them to move to the next level of study. However, it rejects Bloom's idea (lovely but unrealistic) that all (or even most) students can be brought to genuine mastery of a subject. Instead, it defines both adequacy and excellence within a context of interest, aptitude, prior preparation, and purpose. We do not have to buy any one approach hook, line, and sinker. Just as we can find suitable uses for behavioral objectives, we can find and use a powerful nucleus of mastery learning.

A second comment on our method should be made with respect to the "minimal" course some students completed. I have already argued strongly against the present widespread practice of offering pseudo-algebra courses. Was our minimal course a course in pseudo-algebra? Not quite. First, students had to pass the basics in each unit they studied, and we were careful in identifying those basics. Second, we were frank in telling them that if they chose to follow the minimal course of study, they would not be fully prepared for a 4th year of academic math. If at a later time, they felt the need for that 4th year, they would need further preparation. Offering the minimal course was a way of helping students who had trouble with math to complete the requirements for admission to the state university, where, we believed, they would study subjects other than math.

Success must be evaluated in context. What *must* a student know to handle the next material? Teachers should work on this material; for students to succeed with it, teachers may have to omit advanced problems and much material that more interested students need. That procedure can be highly effective within a particular course. However, within the school day as a whole, students should never be deprived of art, music, drama, discussions of everyday ethics, or physical education so that more time can be given to math and reading. Within each academic area, we should work with students on their own level. It is all well and good to say that all students should be taught together and expected to reach the same standards, but it is just not sensible when we are talking about widely different aptitudes and interests. There should be many opportunities for kids to work together, but there must also be intensive attention to individual problems and progress. At the high school level, if students must complete 3 years of academic mathematics even though they hate math and will never use it, teachers do a good job if such students pass an honest minimal course. Students should be encouraged and helped to do an adequate job in, say, math and set free to follow their passion in literature, history, or art. In contrast, the same course for mathematically gifted students would be impoverished; these students would be cheated by such a course. Excellence must be judged in context.

As we saw earlier, John Gardner said much the same thing in his popular work on excellence. However, in the first edition, he suggested strongly that schools should concentrate on academic excellence even though many students would experience failure. He wanted excellent plumbers to be recognized in the adult community, but he did not see it as the school's job to provide a form of education at which the plumber-to-be could succeed. In the revised edition, he wisely agreed with much that James Conant had said earlier about the strength of comprehensive high schools in a democratic society.

We can see how important it is to construct strong curricula before establishing performance standards. As we create various curricula, we should ask whether each contains those skills, concepts, and appreciations that we would like all to acquire. There is no reason why a good vocational course cannot encourage students to engage in problem solving, critical thinking, the study and practice of citizenship, and aesthetic appreciation. These matters are not inherently and exclusively found in traditional academic courses.

OPPORTUNITY-TO-LEARN STANDARDS

"Opportunity-to-learn standards define the availability of programs, staff, and other resources that schools, districts, and states provide so that students are able to meet challenging content and performance standards" (Ravitch, 1995, p. 13). Ravitch comments that such standards have always been the province of the states, and federal officials and legislators are reluctant to intervene in them. This is an unconvincing reason for federal abstinence on these standards. After all, the federal government is intruding in a heavy-handed way on both content and performance standards, both of which have been established by states and even local districts in the past. Many of us believe, skeptically if not cynically, that the government prefers to lay down mandates that it can avoid paying for. Defensible opportunity-to-learn standards would of necessity be expensive.

The first thing to consider here is that it may be impossible to provide equal opportunities to learn if we restrict our thinking to the school context. To give all children a fair chance at both learning and life, a just society would have to tackle social ills that the United States has been slow to address. Without such a national social policy, talk of opportunity-to-learn standards is weak if not empty. Shouting "All children can learn" and "No excuses" will not get us very far.

I am not arguing that we should throw up our hands and accept defeat in the absence of attempts to relieve large social ills. This problem, like so many others we are considering here, does not call for an either/or decision. We must do what we can within schools to provide equal opportunities to learn. On a visit to a wealthy private school in New York City, I had an opportunity to chat with faculty members. One woman told me that her son taught in a public school about a mile away. Whereas she had a wealth of resources in her school, her son and his students started the school year without desks and chairs! In any given year, they never had enough textbooks to supply one for each student.

Jonathan Kozol has been telling us of such conditions for more than 40 years, and yet the conditions still exist. As citizens, we must put pressure on states and cities to equalize resources in schools but, as we do this, we should realize that the equalization of resources in schools may not produce a rise in test scores. Indeed, taxpayers all over the country complain about a lack of improvement in test scores despite hefty increases in funding. Knowing what we do about the effects of family income, housing, and neighborhoods, this should not surprise us. Well, then, some citizens grumble, if providing equal resources doesn't increase learning, why bother? The answer to that should be obvious to anyone with a grain of moral sense: We should do it because it is the decent thing to do. We should not tolerate schools for other people's children that we would not accept for our own.

We could try a number of remedies within schools. We could, for example, provide full-service schools—schools that include dental clinics, social services, infant care, parenting programs, and vision and health clinics on the school campus. We could establish public school boarding arrangements during the school week for children whose families have difficulty getting them to school. We could provide significant salary incentives for good teachers willing to teach in our urban schools. At present, we suffer from shortsightedness, lack of imagination, and an inclination toward simplistic solutions.

NCLB makes a limp effort in the direction of opportunity-to-learn standards by insisting that all classes must be taught by qualified teachers. What it means to be qualified is left for the states to decide, and at present, *qualified* means "certified" or "having the appropriate credential." For the most part, we again avoid the deeper questions about what teachers should know and be able to do. It would take us too far afield to discuss this matter in the required depth, but consider just one oddity. U.S. policymakers constantly deplore the fact that Asian students achieve higher math scores than American students. But we remain remarkably unaffected by differences in the way teachers are prepared in, say, China and the United States. Chinese teachers are prepared in depth on the material they will teach. Elementary school teachers may not take courses in higher mathematics, but they do study the foundations of arithmetic in some depth. In contrast, American educators seem to believe that better preparation requires longer and higher sequences of courses in math. "Methods" courses—the best of which approximate the Chinese model—are held in scorn. To make matters worse, we insist on roughly the same disciplinary training for elementary and secondary school teachers. Both are expected to complete a BA in a recognized discipline. But of what use is a major in literature to the 5th-grade teacher who must teach math, science, and history as well as English? Again, it seems that we would like to solve a pressing problem without really thinking about it. Just put "highly qualified" teachers in every classroom.

NCLB might be given credit for urging schools to employ only qualified teachers, but its manner of enforcing this standard destroys most of its positive effects. Schools are required to inform parents if their child's teacher is not fully qualified. Think what this does to parent–teacher relations, to a teacher's morale, to her students' confidence in her. In this book's last chapter, I'll say more about the deplorable level of moral thinking exhibited in NCLB.

The states are complicit with the federal government on these issues and the absurd solutions written into law. They have too often gutted their curricula by adopting sets of "standards" instead of a set of carefully worked out courses of study, complete with educational aims to guide both specific content selection and pedagogy. They have established complicated lists of competencies and dispositions to credential teachers instead of analyzing the host of teaching situations and how preparation for them might differ. And too many have decided that children have an equal opportunity to learn if they are all forced to take the same subjects. We have reverted to the thinking of the Committee of Ten: There is just one set of material that defines what it means to be educated and, if children are required to study that material, they enjoy equal opportunity to learn. We should be ashamed.

In this chapter, we have discussed the current use of standards to specify content, performance, and opportunity to learn. I have suggested that the pervasive use of detailed instructional objectives directed toward a specific standard for all students has great dangers for real learning and the development of intellectual habits of mind. Instead, I have argued strongly for variable standards, standards that fit subject matter and student aptitudes, interests, and purposes. In the absence of such variation, the use of high-stakes tests makes the situation even more miseducative. We turn next to the topic of testing.

6

TESTING

I N THIS SHORT chapter, I will discuss three important aspects of the current high-stakes testing movement that should worry us. First, the overemphasis on testing and the use of test scores as the main measure of accountability may actually undermine the development and exercise of intellectual habits of mind. Second, the practice of retaining children in grade or refusing to grant high school diplomas on the basis of failing test scores is ill considered and risks great damage to a significant number of students. Third, defining accountability in terms of test scores encourages cheating and is enormously wasteful.

TESTING AND INTELLECTUAL GROWTH

Standardized tests were created and widely used in the 20th century, and most of the tests used to measure IQ, aptitude, and achievement were norm referenced. Norm-referenced tests are used to evaluate where students stand with respect to other test-takers on whatever qualities or skills are being measured. On such tests, by definition, 10% of students will be in the top decile, 10% in the bottom decile, and so on. IQ tests—tests designed to measure general intelligence—are of this sort, and so are the SAT, the GRE (Graduate Record Exam), and the Iowa Test of Basic Skills.

The history of the SAT is instructive for present purposes. The test was, as noted earlier, first called the Scholastic Aptitude Test, and ostensibly it was designed to identify academically talented students, who might, as a result, be encouraged to go to college. Its use represented an important attempt to open college admission to talented students from less wealthy homes. Its general use grew rapidly, however, and it soon became a requirement for admission to many colleges and universities. The SAT became another case of good intentions gone wrong. Critics asserted that the test did not really measure academic aptitude and that there was (there still is) an uncanny correlation between family income and students' scores on the test. In response, the SAT was renamed the Scholastic Assessment Test, but that title has built-in redundancy. Today, it is just the SAT, and the only letter that stands for anything is the *T* for test.

As more and more students from families that can afford it have begun to secure tutoring and take the test two or three times to improve their scores, it has become clear that the test is now even more a measure of family income. Some colleges have stopped requiring the SAT for admission, and many more may follow.

The standardized tests used regularly in schools (tests mandated by NCLB) are more often criterion-referenced tests; that is, the scores represent attainment of specific criteria, not percentile ranking with respect to other scores. A passing score is set at a particular level, and at least theoretically, all students might score at or above that level. Indeed, that is exactly what is demanded by NCLB—that, by 2014, all students will score at the "proficient" level in math and reading.

But how is the score for proficiency to be established? Most states have fallen back on norm-referenced thinking to establish a level of proficiency. We cannot hope to bring all children to the level of, say, the top 10%, but perhaps (a big assumption) we can bring everyone to the level of the top 60%, and so the criterion score is set at that point. Why think this way? What should constitute "passing" and why? The ideal would be to determine the score at which students might be assured of predictable success in future work or study, but we are a long way from having such information, and few policymakers are even asking the question.

Once the level of proficiency is set, schools must work hard to bring their students to that level. This means, of course, that effort is directed at first bringing a certain percentage of students to that score, and then increasing the percentage in each succeeding year. Each state has established its own projected line of improvement (approved by the federal Department of Education), and strategies for constructing the line differ widely. Some states have drawn a straight line from their current percentage of proficient students to the desired 100% in 2014. Others have used a broken line with a small slope in the first years and a steep slope nearing the 2014 mark. One does not have to be a cynic to believe that states using the latter strategy are depending on the collapse or drastic revision of NCLB before the crunch comes.

Even if the expectations laid down by NCLB are ridiculous, it is possible that trying to meet them might accomplish great improvement in student achievement. But spending long hours preparing for tests is not likely to advance genuine achievement, and it may even discourage the growth of intellectual habits of mind. I cannot prove that intellectual habits of mind are being damaged by the overemphasis on tests, but I think it is a potentially great risk.

Over the past 2 years, I have asked a number of recent college graduates this question: What are the angles of a 3-4-5 triangle? The question was inspired by an incident at a conference for Florida high school honor students who had mentored younger students. Governor Jeb Bush attended the conference to honor the young people, and one of them challenged him with this question from the state test. It was unfair to the governor because, of course, the question on the actual test was in multiple-choice form and, given the possible answers, he might have answered correctly. As it was, he stumbled badly. The student, triumphant, responded that she knew the answer—30-60-90—but she was wrong. All of the students I've tried this on (about 20 so far), all graduates of good universities, have gotten it wrong.

Now I urge readers not to skip the next few comments with a shudder— "Math, yuck," "How could I remember such a thing?" and the like. If you went to high school and took an ordinary course in geometry, you should be able at least to follow the story. (If you cannot, why are we teaching this material?) In every case, my young visitors replied, 30-60-90, but I explained that this could not be right because in that triangle the side opposite the 30-degree angle is half the hypotenuse, and 3 is clearly more than half of 5. Then another student said, "Well, maybe 45-45-90?" and I pointed out that such a triangle would be isosceles, and this one was not. I spent some time proving that the answer could not be 30-60-90, reminding them of what happens when you bisect an angle in an equilateral triangle to obtain two 30-60-90 triangles. At the end of all this, one young man who had been accepted to graduate school in a science mumbled, "I still think it has to be 30-60-90."

What accounts for this kind of thinking? We could explore many possibilities, but my suspicion is that these young people are conditioned to believe that you should know the answer to a question on a standardized test. You should *know* it, not have to figure it out. And what special right triangles have they encountered? Yes: 30-60-90 and 45-45-90, and so one of these must be the answer.

We could spend time now on a fascinating lesson developed around this question. (Old math teachers never give up.) I will just point out that if the question had been asked of seventh or eighth graders and they had graph paper and a protractor at hand, these youngsters would probably have drawn the triangle, measured, and got the right answer. The older students, convinced that their memories should produce the answer, were helpless. Increased emphasis on tests might well aggravate this tendency.

I could give many more examples. The worry should be clear. Over-emphasis on tests may work against curiosity and thinking. We already have considerable evidence that too much attention to grades has a similar effect. Concerned for their grade point averages (GPAs), many students have lost most of their intellectual curiosity and are reluctant to take intellectual risks. If I am right on this, our schools and nation may *really* be at risk, but not for the reasons claimed in 1983.

Perhaps, however, it is not faulty instruction that leads to such thoughtless responses but, rather, the form of the question. Questions on multiple-choice tests tend to elicit an "I should know this" response. Suppose we asked the question this way: "How would you find or approximate the angles of a 3-4-5 triangle? Describe various ways you might approach this problem." Now students are being asked to think, and several interesting answers might emerge. This is precisely the sort of evaluation task that cannot be accomplished by multiple-choice testing.

I want to give one more example that illustrates the pedagogical need for time and discussion. A mathematics teacher at a community college told me this story recently. In her remedial math class, one student expressed bewilderment because the answer 5/4 was accepted. She could agree to 1¼ and to 1.25, but 5/4 shook her. The teacher gave this a lot of thought and, while working on another problem, experienced an epiphany of sorts: "Oh, you're thinking of the slash in 5/4 as calling for an operation—5 divided by 4!" The student agreed with relief: 5/4 couldn't be an answer; it was a problem. This student had never been introduced to fractions as rational numbers and had never practiced locating them on a number line. For her, as for most fifth graders, a fraction was "part of a thing." The teacher then spent some time with the class, counting by fourths, thirds, and so on. A whole new world opened up. Again, neither the diagnosis nor the creative lesson would have been produced by a multiple-choice test.

HIGH STAKES

I am not against standardized tests, used judiciously. Indeed, on a personal level, I owe my career in part to having been an exceptionally good test-taker. But many bright, creative people are not good test-takers, and children develop at different rates. I would, therefore, use standardized tests in a positive way—to identify potentially outstanding academic talent and to be sure that instruction is, roughly, on course.

Tests should be used to help, not to penalize students. Retention in grade, for example, rarely helps students. Imagine the emotional agony that a youngster goes through when he or she is forced to repeat 4th grade three times. This is cruel and unnecessary. As I pointed out earlier, in sound mathematical instruction, we try to avoid cumulative ignorance, but we do it by carefully diagnosing the problem, providing special instruction in the areas of difficulty, and then retesting. This is done over a short period of time and a limited range of skills or knowledge. But such a procedure requires us to recognize at the outset of instruction that the range of achievement will be wide. Some students will have to take far more time than others to complete a unit of work, even if they are assigned to a smaller version of the unit. It also forces us to study our subjects carefully. Exactly what must a student be able to do in order to move on to the next unit of study? This is a profound and much neglected question.

Being held back on one test is not a terrible blow, especially if the repetition comes with a promise of ultimate success and of sincere respect for the student's actual interests. Retention in grade, in contrast, can be devastating to the emotional well-being of students, and it is pedagogically counterproductive. We have to leave open the possibility that in rare cases it accomplishes something positive. Not often.

Advocates of high-stakes standardized testing have pointed out that candidates must pass such tests if they want to become lawyers, doctors, nurses, airline pilots, or teachers. Therefore, they argue, kids must get used to these tests, and they need the practice that K–12 schooling now provides. But they fail to note that all of these licensing tests are voluntary. We are not forced to become lawyers, doctors, nurses, airline pilots, or teachers. We study, work hard, and take such tests because we want to enter a particular profession. We have specific goals in mind. School tests, in contrast, are coercive, and there is little evidence that the material tested is really necessary to qualify as a fifth grader or high school graduate.

Even if we accept the "practice" argument, we should remove the high stakes from standardized tests. Working on tests cooperatively, pursuing questions in some depth, and trying to enter the mind of the test-maker are all interesting activities. Kids can even enjoy taking timed tests, competing against themselves for better performances. Tests can, thus, be used as games and as springboards for genuine investigation.

Some advocates of high-stakes tests, however, claim that students will not take the tests seriously unless high stakes are attached. When this happens, there is something very wrong in school relationships. Where relations of care and trust have been formed, kids will usually engage with some enthusiasm in activities suggested by their teacher. There is no educationally defensible reason to impose high-stakes testing on children. The practice simply contributes to the further degradation of relationships.

The tests mandated by NCLB involve high stakes not only for students but also for teachers, administrators, and whole schools. There should be high stakes attached to real incompetence; documented incompetence should result in dismissal, and unusually low scores on a standardized test regularly used can certainly provide some documentation of incompetence. But it is unrealistic and unsympathetic to demand that a school whose students have turned in low scores for years should suddenly—"No excuses!"—produce acceptable scores. Situations of this sort demand careful diagnosis, creative thinking, and realistic planning. For all of these activities, educators should be held accountable; that is, they should be expected to report on the activities and their expected effects. Financial help should be made available for the enactment of plans that are judged feasible. Such help might be provided for smaller classes, new (or varied) text materials for experimental use, creation of research teams combining district and university investigators, and teacher education symposia. Steady improvement should be expected—not miracles.

Accountability should be a regular expectation, but it should be firmly anchored in responsibility, and educators must be responsible for more than test scores. If social interactions, teacher–student relations, school attendance, curiosity and enthusiasm, cooperation, safety, and school pride are all positive or improving, schools should be credited with meeting important responsibilities. Almost certainly, these responsibilities are best encouraged by intelligent support, not by the threats, shame, and penalties that now accompany high-stakes testing.

Another argument for frequent testing (but not with high stakes attached) focuses on the diagnostic value of tests. Well-designed quizzes of the sort given frequently by classroom teachers may have this value. As I argued earlier, good teachers want to identify and provide remedies for faulty learning before students fall badly behind. But standardized tests almost never serve this function. The usual response when students fail the high school exit test in, say, 10th grade is to assign the students to a special test preparation class where all students slog through the same material with no individual diagnosis whatever.

There are powerful diagnostic strategies that teachers might use, and they do not require standardized tests. One such strategy (one I have used in teaching mathematics) is so-called overt thinking, a tool used by many psychologists. The teacher, working with one student, starts a session by presenting a problem or task, saying to the student, "Let me hear you think." This is scary at first, but as students become aware that their thinking will often be complimented ("You're going great") they may actually look forward to such sessions. The strategy has the great merit of following the student's initiative, interrupting only to point out errors. The central feature of this technique is critical listening, and critical listening requires dialogue. The community college teacher who recognized the nature of her student's difficulty with the notation 5/4 did so by persisting in dialogue, and then thinking critically about the student's responses.

The strategy also contributes to the construction of powerful lessons. My discussion with students about the 3-4-5 triangle has generated pages of rich, fascinating math lessons. Understanding the student's dilemma with "5/4" also led to valuable lessons with that class, a commitment to future lessons, and vital advice to elementary school teachers. Thus the best diagnostic tools also contribute to pedagogical methods.

Here is another example (partly true and partly fiction): A high school English teacher was teaching a familiar topic—subject and predicate—to students who had great difficulty with reading and writing.

> TEACHER: Now look at this sentence: *Dan finished his algebra homework last night*. What is the subject?
> STUDENT: Algebra.
> TEACHER: Hmm. Well, try this: *Dan finished his homework last night*. Now, what's the subject?
> STUDENT: It's still probably algebra, but it doesn't say.

The teacher in this case understood part of the student's difficulty. As some students laughed at the confused student, the teacher hushed them, turned to the dictionary, and proved to the class that *subject* often accurately refers to a school subject. Indeed, she began to build a series of lessons on the meaning of *subject*. One of those meanings, of course, is the one that was wanted here—a syntactic meaning. Moving carefully, the teacher encouraged students to consider some other sentences:

> Dan finished his homework.
> The cat pounced on a mouse.
> The sky turned dark.
> Flying a kite is fun.

As she moved from easily identifiable agents as subjects to entities to which various attributes are ascribed, to participle phrases, the teacher became more deeply aware of just how difficult the topic (or *subject*) really is. She moved slowly and spent considerable time locating the usual mistakes in failure of agreement. The students had fun with this and agreed that writing clearly required such agreement. At the end of these lessons, the teacher had begun to rethink the whole business of teaching subject and predicate. She had found a better way to approach the teaching of writing.

The point here is that standardized tests are not very helpful in diagnosis, and unless we isolate an interesting question now and then and devote time to it, they are likely to mislead us in constructing lessons. The teacher discussed above devised a whole week's lessons around the various meanings of *subject*. In many schools today, she would not have been allowed to do this because these lessons were not part of the official curriculum. What a waste of teacher creativity!

WASTE AND CORRUPTION

Much energy is wasted today on trivial exercises and tests that may undermine intellectual growth. But in addition to the frightening waste of intellectual potential, enormous expenditures of time and money are made on tests—their construction, constant revision, administration, security, scoring, analysis, and reporting. In some districts, tests are delivered by security services and meticulously counted at both office and classroom sites before and after administration. Heaven forbid that a test should go missing! Everything would have to be redone. It would seem far more reasonable to cut testing programs drastically and use the funds saved to finance promising programs of instruction, smaller classes, instructional aides, or even campus beautification.

There is some evidence that the current overemphasis on testing is causing corruption as well as waste (Nichols & Berliner, 2007). Not only is there more student cheating but there are also more cases of cheating by sympathetic teachers and desperate administrators. Not long ago, a student in one of my graduate classes spoke angrily about the overemphasis on standardized tests, particularly those with high stakes. As the discussion proceeded, he claimed that teachers who help their students on the tests by pointing to errors and correct answers are justified in doing so. "It's civil disobedience," he asserted. I encouraged the students to think more deeply about this. Such cheating cannot be construed as civil disobedience. Why not?

This is another case that illustrates the value of dialogue and analysis. As we explored the issue, we had an opportunity to think about civil disobedience. The key element in civil disobedience is the willingness of those who commit it to do so publicly and to incur the consequences of breaking the law. To set a moral example, to promote a just cause, those who commit civil disobedience go to jail, lose jobs, and sometimes suffer persecution. They do not cheat. Cheating damages the whole web of care and weakens our efforts to maintain relations of care and trust. If NCLB has a corrupting influence, it should be rethought. Any law that makes good people bad and bad people worse is a bad law. It should be repealed or revised.

We need accurate figures on the costs of our overindulgence on testing. What else could we do with this money? A cost-benefit analysis is in order. But even if some benefits (higher test scores) are achieved through high-stakes testing, moral questions remain. Are we willing to do morally questionable things to raise test scores? I'll return to moral questions in the concluding chapter.

In this chapter, I have raised several questions about the overuse of standardized testing and, especially, about high-stakes testing: Does the overemphasis on testing risk undermining intellectual growth? Is it morally acceptable to motivate people with threats, shame, and penalties? Is retention in grade justified? If standardized tests are not useful for diagnostic purposes, are there other strategies we might use? Is the overuse of standardized tests encouraging waste and corruption?

7

CHOICE

C HOICE (OR FREEDOM) is a central concept in liberal philosophy and a basic element in any liberal democracy. Given its centrality in democratic life, it is puzzling that practice in making intelligent choices gets so little attention in public schools. Today, when people speak of choice in connection with education, they usually have in mind *parental* choice, and they may advocate a system of vouchers to accommodate this choice. I argue that this mode of choice might well undermine, rather than advance, democratic life. In contrast, providing opportunities for students to make well-informed, age-appropriate choices concerning their own education in our public schools might well strengthen both personal responsibility and our democracy.

SCHOOL CHOICE

The idea of providing vouchers for families to spend on schools of their own choice has not, so far, become popular with American citizens, but the idea is certainly not dead. The argument for such a plan is unconvincing on several counts. First, its advocates often claim that with vouchers, poor parents could make the kind of choices open to only the rich in the past. Now, the argument runs, with vouchers, poor parents can also choose the schools they want their children to attend. This is ludicrous. Wealthy parents often pay more than $30,000 a year for the school of their choice. Poor parents would have to manage with a fraction of this.

73

Second, the schools sought by wealthy parents are usually well established and often well endowed. Wealthy parents do not have to worry that their childrens' schools will be closed because of financial problems or, worse, academic shortcomings. Advocates of vouchers even tout the strength of a market system that would close down failing schools—not the rich, well-established schools, of course. It is easy to talk about closing schools just as the market "closes" businesses that can't compete. But a school is not a business. A school, properly, is a child's second home—a place of security, social interaction, and intellectual stimulation. To close down this special place is to do great injury in a child's life. And suppose that children are informed in, say, the middle of 4th grade that their school will close at the end of the year. Do voucher advocates have any understanding of what this might mean to children? What do the harried and disappointed parents do? Closing a school is not like closing a gas station or corner market, and even these closings can cause hardship.

Third, it is likely that under a voucher system, many parents would choose schools sponsored by religious institutions. Using their own money, they have a right to do this, although some careful thinkers have argued that our laws should never have allowed it. Today the question is whether public money should be provided for such a choice. I feel strongly that this would be a very dangerous move. If we had started out, as some other modern states did, with a dual system of public-Catholic, public-Lutheran, or public-Anglican schools, all publicly financed, our democracy might be relatively safe. But in our enormously diverse society, where would we draw the line? Should parents be allowed, for example, to send their children at public expense to schools that insist on the subordination of women? Some respectable political philosophers have argued courageously against even Catholic schools on this criterion. Many religious schools endorse ideas and practices that reject or weaken the social agenda of liberal democracies. Citizens are and should be free to argue against any part of such a social agenda, but the liberal state itself should not be asked to fund practices that oppose its agenda. Neither, I hasten to add, should problematic elements of that agenda be taught dogmatically in public schools. Balance, debate, and critical thinking should be the watchwords in publicly funded schools.

There is another reason to insist that public money be directed only to public schools. Traditionally, the public schools have stood between parents and state, guided (imperfectly, granted) by local communities. Under this system, neither parent nor state owns the child. It is hard to exaggerate the importance of this role played by public schools. By regularly involving parents in decisions on curriculum, administration, and extracurricular activities, a democratic society avoids the threat of state control over its schools. But the state plays a role—legislating against discriminatory practices, suggesting valuable alternatives for curriculum, disseminating information on promising practices, and regulating financial management. Under such a system, the child should be safe from the tyranny of either parent or state.

Some choice is provided within the public schools under NCLB. Parents are supposed to be informed if their child's school is on the "needs improvement" list; such schools have failed to make AYP at least 2 years in a row. Under the provisions of NCLB, such parents are to be informed that they may transfer their children to a better performing school in the district. This sounds fine. But suppose all or most of a district's schools are on the list? Suppose the "better" schools that do exist are on the opposite side of the city? This is likely to be the case, since test scores and economic status are so closely linked. Or suppose, as often happens, the better schools are already filled up? The choice provided by NCLB is largely a well-intended but false promise.

REAL CHOICE

The public school as a major institution in a democratic society should be a place where children learn to make intelligent, well-informed choices. It is baffling that this obligation is so seldom taken seriously. Perhaps liberal educators and policymakers have agreed with John Stuart Mill that liberty and choice are not meant for children and "barbarians," both of whom need to be directed and controlled. However, liberal thinkers such as John Dewey have argued that people need practice in making age-appropriate choices if they are to be prepared for life in a free society. Schools must, then, provide opportunities for students to make well-informed choices.

This is one key to removing the harm done by assigning students to tracks on the basis of test scores or past school performance. The record of tracking in the United States is a shameful one. The comprehensive high school, with its several tracks designed to accommodate different talents and interests, should have been a resounding success. In some ways, as we saw, it has been successful. The idea is a good one, but its implementation has been faulty. The key is to allow students to choose their own course of study.

The choice should be well-informed. Guidance and discussion about high school courses should start early and continue into the high school years. Test scores and performance records should be used in a positive way to reassure those who are doing well and to give supportive warning to those who have not done well and may experience difficulty under the choice they are considering. Students who want to take an academic course of study should be allowed to do so, and extra time and help should be made available to them. No student should be assigned to a track against his or her will. (And yes, that means he or she should not be manipulated, sweet-talked, or frightened into it.)

But tracks other than the academic track should be made rich and attractive, and this is the second key to removing the shameful legacy of a good idea. It should be possible for youngsters to choose proudly any course of study the school offers. It is time to show the respect for diversity that we so easily talk about.

There are signs that such a move might soon receive some attention. Various individuals and groups are discussing a new concept of universal education, one that emphasizes values and process skills over subject matter knowledge. Lists of such attributes include speaking and listening skills, flexibility in the face of change, critical thinking, social skills and ability to work in teams, acceptance of personal responsibility, creativity, and willingness to engage in problem solving. Note that all of these attributes can be nurtured in any track or course. They are not the exclusive property of the traditional disciplines.

There are at least two questionable beliefs supporting the present insistence on preparing everyone for college. One is the seemingly generous claim that "all children can learn," which is about as meaningful as "all children can eat." Of course, all children can (must) eat, but they cannot all eat everything we might offer and, in many cases, they could (without harm) eat offered foods that they simply refuse. We need not push the analogy further, but we should recognize that "all children can learn" means nothing until we say what it is that "they" can learn.

After many years of experience, I do not believe that all children can learn algebra to a level we might properly regard as proficient. Am I an irredeemable elitist? I am not. I respect and admire all sorts of talent, and I believe that no child's self-esteem or status in democratic schooling should depend on his or her proficiency in mathematics. I do not want to concentrate on a child's deficiencies in academic math and their remediation. Rather, I want to find out what the child might be good at and, then, ask how our schools might develop and encourage this talent.

I want children to have sufficient time to explore and find out what they might be good at. To do that, they should be exposed to algebra and to any other subject we have long defended, but they should not be expected to "pass" it or meet uniform standards set for it. The middle school years should provide the opportunity for such exploration, and much time in those years should be spent on discussion, guidance, and trying things out.

Critics oppose such suggestions by pointing (as Mill did) to the immaturity of schoolchildren. Children do not know what they need, and we, as responsible adults, should know and insist that they learn what they will need. Suppose, after a year or several years, a boy in a vocational program wants to go to college. But he has not taken the required preparatory courses. Now what? Now he should switch programs and be supported in doing so. Perhaps he will need an extra year of preparation, maybe even two. This experience, too, may well become part of the new universal education. Midcareer changes in adult life are frequent, and flexibility in the face of change is one of the attributes emphasized in the new universal education. If during his time in a vocational program, the boy has acquired learning skills, positive attitudes toward work, a capacity for critical thinking, and increased intellectual curiosity, he may be well prepared for the change.

The second questionable belief that supports a uniform subject matter curriculum for everyone is that only certain, well established disciplines serve as appropriate preparation for college. One must study academic biology, not the sort of popular science that most people will depend upon for health and informed citizenship through a lifetime. One must study algebra, not the practical mathematics that will be useful in daily life. And one must study formal grammar, instead of practicing, with continuous guidance, the kind of spoken English that will prove persuasive in a job interview.

This questionable belief has spawned a brood of related, equally questionable beliefs. One is the odd notion that great literature can only be studied in a course on great literature. Is it impossible for kids in a vocational program to read Dickens's *Hard Times*, Sinclair Lewis's *Babbitt*, some Tolstoy, and perhaps even Hardy's *Jude the Obscure*? If the idea is preposterous, why does it become reasonable that the same kids will read these books profitably in a standard English course?

Closely related to the belief that traditional courses are the proper home for great literature is the notion that the great standard works—the canon—will somehow automatically induce critical thinking. Treated well, they might. Those of us who love great literature cannot imagine life without it, but it is not the only path to critical thinking, and coerced and taught pedantically, it may turn away many students. They become adults who rarely read a book. It would surely be better to integrate great books, current works, and practical articles into courses wherever they are relevant. This holds not only across programs—that is, for vocational as well as academic programs—but also across disciplines. Math students should be given opportunities to read Jacque Hadamard's *The Psychology of Invention in the Mathematical Field*, Edwin Abbott's *Flatland*, and Martin Gardner's

Annotated Alice (the annotated version of Lewis Carroll's *Alice's Adventures in Wonderland*), as well as portions of E. T. Bell's *Men of Mathematics*.

Real choice—the liberty so cherished in Western democracies—should be encouraged early and in every aspect of education. To make such choice a reality, schools will have to become flexible in their organization, time requirements, and evaluation procedures. But if the new universal education seeks flexibility as an attribute of its students, we can hardly expect less of the schools that will educate them.

Before closing this chapter, we should mention again the important role of extracurricular activities in promoting choice and the skills for democratic living. Too often, policymakers cut these programs in the interest of enhancing "real" studies in the disciplines. Such economies are shortsighted. Clubs, teams, and performing groups all provide fruitful opportunities for students to engage in democratic processes and to learn genuine respect for people whose talents and interests may be different from their own. They are vital for democratic education.

In this chapter, I have contrasted current views of school choice that give parents more power in choosing their children's schools with genuine, democratic choice for students within our public schools. This second pattern of choice is more compatible with democratic life, and it may well help to establish a new, 21st century concept of universal education.

8

THE MORAL
OF THE STORY

MOST REFORM movements, paradoxically, have been flawed by moral shortcomings. The comprehensive high school—an astounding success in many ways—has been deeply flawed by its coercive and morally repugnant practice of assigning kids (disproportionately minority) to non-academic tracks and providing poor courses to those in the "lower" tracks. I've argued that the main flaw can be removed by allowing choice, providing continuous guidance, and creating rich and relevant courses. The math/science reforms of the 1960s were defective in their failure to consider the whole population of students and, again, in contributing to the compartmentalization of subjects. The sensible remedy here is to revisit some promising conceptual structures and see how they might be reconstituted and broadened for particular segments of the school population.

Like so many reform movements, NCLB and its immediate predecessors started on the moral high ground—an expressed intention to close the achievement gap. But almost everything that followed by way of planning and implementation reveals a shocking level of moral obtuseness. If the consequences we are seeing now had been anticipated (as they should have been), how might the law have been written? The consequences most to be deplored include increased fear and anxiety in students; the demoralization of many good teachers; a possible increase in the dropout rate (we are not yet sure about this); increased corruption among students, teachers, and administrators; an impoverished curriculum lacking in depth, connections, and exposure to the arts; and an emphasis on testing that may actually make the development of intellectual habits of mind less likely.

The move from an emphasis on inputs to one on outcomes (or outputs) might be morally justified. Educators should use resources in a way that is reasonably thought likely to produce the outcomes sought, and the government should be assured that its money is not wasted. But there is a huge territory between inputs (financial and intellectual resources) and outcomes (test scores). That territory is the whole, ongoing school life of students and teachers. It is not just educational ends that must be morally justified; our means must also pass a moral test. If the means chosen cause sleeplessness and nausea, increased boredom, poorer relationships, reduced thinking, and lower creativity, they must be rejected. Further, we should not forsake interest in inputs. Intellectual inputs represent opportunities. We should, as teachers, present possibilities—not only demands for specific learning outcomes. What we offer is every bit as important as what we demand.

I would like to see NCLB repealed. We should start over. But corruption has not resulted in violence and murder in the streets as it did with Prohibition, so perhaps we should aim only for revision. What might that revision include? In addition to revising the law, the Department of Education should consider ways to support schools and educational researchers in their efforts to achieve a new vision for future education, and I'll suggest some points to consider. Let's start, however, with the necessary revisions:

1. *The requirement for 100% proficiency in reading and math should be abandoned.* It is not right to mandate the impossible. AYP should also be dropped entirely. Instead, the law should ask for evidence of steady improvement over a period of, say, 5 years. This would give schools time to plan and monitor their programs, and it would give the Department of Education time to watch trends, instead of leaping to punish failures that may be only anomalies. Useful data would be collected over this time period, and states could be warned about districts or particular schools that seem to be in trouble.
2. *The painful and morally questionable federal threats and penalties should be dropped.* It is not right to attempt to motivate people through shame and punishment. We would be rightly offended if teachers treated their students this way. States and districts should decide what to do with low-performing schools. Some such schools may in fact deserve great praise for doing a heroic job even if test scores have not gone up. However, if

a school or district has shown no improvement over 5 years and state officials provide no adequate explanation for the failure and no reasonable plan for improvement, the federal government would be justified in denying further federal funds to that school or district.

A word on the process of reauthorization: As the reauthorization of NCLB is considered, an advisory committee similar to the original one should be appointed, but this time government officials should *listen to the advice it gives.*

It is not just NCLB that needs revision and fresh thinking. The Department of Education should also consider major changes in its entire approach to education. Some suggestions:

1. *Recognize explicitly that education is broader than schooling* and that success in school is largely dependent on social and economic factors over which schools have no control. Promote interagency cooperation to improve conditions of health, housing, parenting, safety, and general well-being.
2. *Recognize explicitly that children are different* in their aptitudes and interest; give up the present faulty and harmful notion of equality as sameness.
3. *Shift attention in research to, or at least expand it to include, research that questions basic premises.* Much research today concentrates on finding "what works" in, for example, teaching everyone algebra. But suppose many people really do not need algebra to lead successful lives? Suppose the guiding premise is wrong? Support research that studies adults in a wide range of occupations. Find out what mathematics they use in their occupational and personal lives. Then fund development of differentiated courses compatible with different occupations and ways of life.
4. *Deemphasize randomized experiments and field trials.* Children and teachers are not atoms, gadgets, or beetles. Support instead the study of reasonable educational experiments to which participants give their enthusiastic assent. But, critics will complain, studies using volunteers are more likely to yield positive results and, therefore they can't tell us what would work for everyone. Yes, exactly. Capitalize on this nugget of wisdom about human beings. We are different. Further, consent and choice are fundamental to democratic life.
5. *Study carefully the preparation of teachers.* Again, question premises. Why, for example, should elementary school teachers be required to take a major in a standard discipline? How will a major in, say, biology

contribute to a teacher's knowledge of the full range of subjects he or she must teach? It might be better for elementary teacher candidates to have 4 years of intensive study in all the subjects taught at the elementary level. This study would, of course, be pitched at a higher and deeper level, but its concentration would be on *what the teacher will teach*. Such teachers would not be prepared for graduate work in a discipline, but they would be prepared for work on the problems of professional teaching.

Does this sound rather like the preparation once provided by teachers' colleges? It does. The idea was not a bad one, but it had dramatic weaknesses, and these can be remedied. The main reason for insisting on a traditional major for elementary school teachers is one of status. We would like teacher candidates to be recognized as equal to other graduates, not as second-class degree holders. (There's that notion of equality as sameness again.) But there is no good reason why a person who has mastered five or six disciplines at a basic level should be considered inferior to someone who has mastered (or barely survived) one traditional major which may have little to do with his/her chosen occupation.

Similarly, the education of secondary school teachers should be re-examined. Some critics have recently recommended (once again, it is not a new idea) that mathematics teachers should have "exactly the same" courses as other math majors. Why? Status again. We should separate status issues from knowledge issues. Mathematics teachers need far broader preparation than math majors who intend to pursue graduate studies in mathematics. They need history, epistemology, aesthetics, a wide range of applications, literature, and biography related to mathematics. They also need interdisciplinary work. There may be nothing we can do about stodgy math professors who scorn every course designed for teachers as "watered down," or worse, "dumbed down." We have to prove them wrong. Meanwhile, by neglecting to question premises, we are failing to discover what may be essential in teacher preparation.

6. *Discourage states and districts from using retention in grade and withholding diplomas* on the basis of test scores. This does not mean embracing "social promotion." It means doing something constructive to help students who are having academic difficulties. It means recognizing research that has shown retention to be harmful. There should be no high stakes attached to standardized test scores for students.

7. *Recognize that children develop at different rates.* Promote programs that allow students more than 4 years to complete high school, but do this through positive planning, not by retention. We should help kids get

through high school, perhaps by carrying a lighter load, perhaps by changing from one program to another. High school graduation not only contributes to a higher lifetime income—it also increases the likelihood that students will pursue further training.

8. *Encourage responsible experimentation designed to increase relations of care and trust.* One possibility is to promote continuity by allowing students and teachers to stay together for, say, 3 years rather than the typical 1 year. At the high school level, a math teacher might see students through their entire math program. This plan should not be mandatory. It should be used by mutual consent, and it should be studied to identify its benefits. In general, plans to establish relations of care and trust should improve (or at least not hurt) achievement, but they also might contribute to greater safety, stronger social ties, better citizenship, and greater satisfaction for both teachers and students.

9. *Encourage the study of new ideas for universal education.* Might it be better to organize our curricula around problems and themes rather than the narrow, traditional disciplines? Is this change in organization required for continuing growth and development? Will it be the education of the future? Are we sliding backward by emphasizing standardization and uniformity when we should be considering new and creative ideas? Again, support studies that question premises.

10. Perhaps most important of all, *restore genuine respect for the full range of human talents and occupations.* Look around at our communities and great cities. We are an interdependent society, and our respect for all honest work and workers has made the America of which we are rightly proud. Not every child needs to go to college, but every child needs an education that will help him or her to find useful, profitable, and enjoyable work and a satisfying personal life.

We need to engage in fresh thinking. The great biologist Edward O. Wilson wrote recently that, in addition to an interdisciplinary focus, "the best approach to general education in the future would seem to be less discipline-oriented and more problem oriented" (2006, p. 136). We should draw back from standardization and outmoded structures of schooling, but remain willing to analyze, adapt, and revise promising old ideas. In the process, we should avoid dehumanizing teachers and students and explore new ways to educate for genuine intellectual growth, moral commitment, and democratic citizenship.

BIBLIOGRAPHY

Adler, M. J. (1982). *The Paideia proposal.* New York: Macmillan.

Angus, D. L., & Mirel, J. E. (1999). *The failed promise of the American high school, 1890–1995.* New York: Teachers College Press.

Berliner, D., & Biddle, B. (1996). *The manufactured crisis: Myths, fraud, and the attack on America's public schools.* New York: Perseus Books.

Bestor, A. (1953). *Educational wastelands: The retreat from learning in our public schools.* Urbana: University of Illinois Press.

Bloom, B. S. (1981). *All our children learning.* New York: McGraw-Hill.

Bracey, G. (1998). *Put to the test: An educator's guide to standardized testing.* Bloomington, IN: Phi Delta Kappa.

Conant, J. B. (1959). *The American high school today: A first report to interested citizens.* New York: McGraw-Hill.

Conant, J. B. (1967). *The comprehensive high school: A second report to interested citizens.* New York: McGraw-Hill.

Darling-Hammond, L. (2004). What happens to a dream deferred? The continuing quest for equal educational opportunity. In J. A. Banks (Ed.), *Handbook of research on multicultural education* (2nd ed., pp. 607–630). San Francisco: Jossey-Bass.

Eliot, C. W. (1905). The fundamental assumptions in the Report of the Committee of Ten. *Educational Review, 30,* 325–343.

Emery, K., & Ohanian, S. (2004). *Why is corporate America bashing our public schools?* Portsmouth, NH: Heinemann.

Gardner, J. W. (1984). *Excellence* (2nd ed.). New York: W. W. Norton. (Original work published 1961)

Howe, K. (1997). *Understanding equal educational opportunity.* New York: Teachers College Press.

Kahne, J. (1996). *Reframing educational policy.* New York: Teachers College Press.

Kliebard, H. (1995). *The struggle for the American curriculum, 1893–1958.* New York: Routledge.

Kliebard, H. (1999). *Schooled to work: Vocationalism and the American curriculum, 1876–1946.* New York: Teachers College Press.

Kohn, A. (2000). *The case against standardized testing.* Portsmouth, NH: Heinemann.

Kohn, A. (2004). *What does it mean to be well educated?* Boston: Beacon Press.

Kozol, J. (1991). *Savage inequalities.* New York: Crown.

Kozol, J. (2005). *The shame of a nation: The restoration of apartheid schooling in America.* New York: Crown.

Meier, D., & Wood, G. (Eds.). (2004). *Many children left behind.* Boston: Beacon Press.

Molnar, A. (1996). *Giving kids the business: The commercialization of America's schools.* Boulder, CO: Westview Press.

National Commission on Excellence in Education. (1983). *A nation at risk.* Washington, DC: U.S. Government Printing Office.

National Commission on Excellence in Education. (1984). *A nation at risk: The full account.* Portland, OR: USA Research.

Nichols, S., & Berliner, D. (2007). *Collateral damage: How high-stakes testing corrupts America's schools.* Cambridge, MA: Harvard Education Press.

Noddings, N. (2003). *Happiness and education.* Cambridge, England: Cambridge University Press.

Noddings, N. (2005). *The challenge to care in schools* (2nd ed.). New York: Teachers College Press.

Noddings, N. (2006). *Critical lessons: What our schools should teach.* Cambridge, England: Cambridge University Press.

Ravitch, D. (1995). *National standards in American education.* Washington, DC: Brookings Institution Press.

Rose, M. (1995). *Possible lives: The promise of public education in America.* Boston: Houghton Mifflin.

Rose, M. (2005). *The mind at work: Valuing the intelligence of the American worker.* New York: Penguin.

Silberman, C. E. (1970). *Crisis in the classroom: The remaking of American education.* New York: Random House.

Spring, J. (2000). *American education.* Boston: McGraw-Hill.

Spring, J. (2003). *Educating the consumer-citizen.* Mahwah, NJ: Lawrence Erlbaum.

Steele, C. M. (1997). A threat in the air: How stereotypes shape intellectual identity and performance. *American Psychologist, 52,* 613–629.

Thayer, Y. V. (1996). The Virginia model: School to community intervention techniques to prevent violence. In A. M. Hoffman (Ed.), *Schools, Violence, and Society* (pp. 275–295). Westport, CT: Praeger.

Tyack, D. (2003). *Seeking common ground: Public schools in a diverse society.* Cambridge: Harvard University Press.

Willis, P. (1977). *Learning to labor.* Farnborough, England: Saxon House.

Wilson, E. O. (2006). *The creation: An appeal to save life on earth.* New York: W. W. Norton.

INDEX

ABOUT THE AUTHOR

Nel Noddings is Lee Jacks Professor of Education Emerita at Stanford University. She is a past president of the National Academy of Education, the Philosophy of Education Society, and the John Dewey Society. In addition to 15 books—among them, *Caring: A Feminine Approach to Ethics and Moral Education, Women and Evil, The Challenge to Care in Schools, Educating for Intelligent Belief or Unbelief,* and *Philosophy of Education*—she is the author of more than 200 articles and chapters. Her latest books are *Starting at Home: Caring and Social Policy, Educating Moral People, Happiness and Education, Educating Citizens for Global Awareness,* and *Critical Lessons: What Our Schools Should Teach.* Noddings spent 15 years as a teacher, administrator, and curriculum supervisor in New Jersey public schools, and served as Director of the Laboratory Schools at the University of Chicago. At Stanford, she received the Award for Teaching Excellence three times.